My Story!
His Song!
Blessed!

SHERMAN ANDRUS SR.

WESTBOW
PRESS®
A DIVISION OF THOMAS NELSON
& ZONDERVAN

WestBow Press books may be ordered through booksellers or by contacting:

WestBow Press
A Division of Thomas Nelson & Zondervan
1663 Liberty Drive
Bloomington, IN 47403
www.westbowpress.com
844-714-3454

ISBN: 978-1-6642-2330-1 (sc)
ISBN: 978-1-6642-2329-5 (e)

Print information available on the last page.

WestBow Press rev. date: 03/29/2021

Contents

Foreword by Pat Boone

God loves singers.

That's just a fact. If you read through the Bible carefully, as I have many times now, you find so much evidence that He loves, hears, enjoys, and actually inspires singers to tell His story and draw people to Him.

We all know David was "a man after God's own heart", though he had flaws and made some grievous mistakes in his life, which God made sure we knew about. But He loved David's singing so much that He preserved most of the Psalms, written and *sung* by David, in His Bible!

In Genesis 4, God lets us know that a grandson of Cain was "the first to play the flute and harp!"

And in the fervid excitement and celebration right after the Israelites emerged on the other side of the Red Sea, having watched God drown the Egyptian army behind them--Moses' sister Miriam led all the women in a spontaneous song on the spot, "Sing to the Lord, for He has triumphed gloriously!"

In 2 Chronicles 20, when King Jehoshaphat cried out to the Lord when confronted by a far superior army, the King appointed singers to march ahead of the army of Israel, singing "Give thanks to the Lord, His faithful love endures forever!" And the larger, better equipped army fell into confusion, and were utterly destroyed, hundreds of thousands of them.

Under the Law of Moses, singers were selected and utilized in worship powerfully, just like the priests who taught and led. In one of the psalms God is described as "singing over us in love."

My point in all this? I consider Sherman Andrus a faithful and powerful servant of our Creator God. We've known and traveled and sung praises to the Lord together over many years. On his own--and as a vital part of The Imperials, a longtime premier Gospel singing group-- he's used his excellent singing ability to honor the Lord and call countless thousands to become Jesus' disciples for decades.

We've traveled the country, my family, and the Imperials, singing and praying and laughing and rejoicing in our Christian lives, and the indescribable fun of knowing we were doing exactly what God wanted us to do!! You can imagine what it meant to me, as a dad of 4 teenage daughters, to be on the road with young men who loved the Lord and encouraged my girls to enjoy singing for Him like they did.

But that's just our part of Sherman's colorful, intriguing life.

Though we shared some important chapters in his life and career--I didn't know all the other chapters he's about to share with you! Like most of us, like most everybody really, he's had his ups and downs, successes, and disappointments, and has come more than once to decision points that would determine where the rest of his life would take him.

If you're not fully aware of his music and his life through the years, I make a prediction right here--once you've read this book, you'll want to seek out all the glorious music he helped create and appreciate the life God led him through as he created it.

I repeat--God loves singers. Especially the ones who devote their talents to Him.

Dedication

"I dedicate this book to the memory of my late son, Sherman Andrus Jr., and to my beautiful wife, Winnie Holman Andrus. *Winnie, you have been my greatest source of support and love, without which I could have done none of this. You have inspired me beyond words. Sherman, the boy who thought I could do anything, grew up to be a fine, accomplished young man! Winnie, you are the love of my life. You've been the greatest supporter and sport, going all over the world with me and helping me make sense of my life as a musician on the road. Thank you for raising our son when I was on the road. Thank you for being my chauffeur on countless road trips! I also dedicate this book to my mom and dad, all my brothers and sisters and many other relatives. There is so much talent in my family, yet you all coalesced behind me and supported me wholeheartedly! I am so thankful for your love and support.*"

Introduction

For many years I have procrastinated about writing a book; not just an autobiography but also a history of Gospel music—of which I have been a part for more than sixty years. I have been a professional singer for more than fifty years. There are so many people I would like to thank and to mention in this book, people who have had an impact on my life. I am getting up there in age and I want to have an opportunity to share with young people, who are now in the Gospel Music business, a little bit of the history from my perspective. Hopefully, my story causes them to be inquisitive about the great artists who have gone before. Currently there is quite a history that Bill Gaither has memorialized through the Gaither videos. Some of the greats were Jake Hess, the Goodman Family and James Blackwood. My hat is off to Mr. Gaither for what he did to provide a living history of Southern Gospel music. We are standing on the shoulders of those artists. I was fortunate to work with three great Gospel groups: Andrae Crouch and The Disciples, The Imperials, and Andrus, Blackwood and Company. We were inspired and influenced by those earlier groups. My personal experience came from black Gospel groups like the Caravans, the Dixie Hummingbirds, the Five Blind Boys of Alabama, and the Five Blind Boys of Mississippi. We also listened to Brother Joe Mayes and Alex Bradford. I don't know if they made a lot of money, but they sure made a great impact on my life! As I listened to the songs they sang, I was inspired to become a Gospel singer. I hope you will have a better understanding about Gospel music and come to see how God led and directed my life as you read further in this book.

Thank you for being a part of my life. I might miss naming some of you, but you all know who you are, and I just thank God for you! I thank you for the prayers, but not only the prayers but also the support that all my fans have provided over the years! I am thankful for my prayer partners and fellow Christians who have walked beside me on this journey. I thank you for all that you have done to bless me and to assist me to fulfill the call of God on my life.

Growing up in Louisiana

World War II began with Nazi Germany's attack on Poland in September 1939. The U.S. did not enter the war until the attack on Pearl Harbor on December 7, 1941. On June 23, 1942, I was born into a world conflicted with war. I was the fifth child born to Simon and Mable Andrus. I was born in Mermentau, Louisiana, a town of 135-140 people. At the time I was born there were two boys and two twin girls, older than me. Later, I would have one more sister and one more brother. My mom lost three children at birth so there were seven of us. As far back as I can remember, I was a happy child. I loved and admired my older brothers and sisters, and they were my heroes.

You may not be aware but at that time there was segregation in the South. Blacks and whites went to different schools and different churches. There were designated places for black people to sit, shop, eat, and yes, to even get a drink of water or go to the restroom. Black people were treated as non-people and did not share the same rights as white people. There was a great racial divide in the country and in the South, racism and discrimination were alive and well.

Despite that, I had a wonderful childhood. It was beautiful! We did so many fun things together. We had a happy family that loved to sing, and we spent lots of time listening to music on the radio. One of the stations we listened to all the time was Hoss Man Allen on station WLAC, Nashville, Tennessee. He played rhythm and blues and gospel. It must have been a fifty-thousand-watt station because we could hear it clearly in Louisiana! It was just a great time!

I guess we were poor, but you couldn't prove it by me or my family. Maybe my older brothers and sisters experienced poverty, but by the time I came along, we were doing quite well. My dad worked at Ziegler's Shipyard in Mermentau. We charged all our groceries at the commissary where he worked. My mom ordered clothes from Alden's and Mervyn Kahn's for me, my sister, and my youngest brother, Calvin. We were living "high on the hog" as they say down south. We were so blessed to be born to such wonderful parents.

My mom was very progressive. We were one of the first families in Mermentau, white or black, to have a telephone or television in our home. We were also one of the first homes with indoor plumbing. I remember having to haul buckets of water from a well that was centrally located in our little town before we had water in our house. Each day after school all the kids would pile into our living room to watch cartoons. My mom was very gracious and welcomed everyone. Many people would call long distance to our house to speak to their mothers, fathers, and other relatives. My mom would dispatch me or Orelia to go find whomever they wanted to talk with and bring them to our house. I remember at one time my mom sent me to get Mr. Green. One of his relatives had called long distance to speak with him. Mr. Green obviously had never used a telephone before, because when my mom directed him to the phone on the desk, he stood in the middle of the room and gave a hearty "Hello!" My mom made me leave the room because I was laughing so hard! After she showed him how to use the phone, she joined me on the porch laughing as hard as I had earlier.

My mom was a prayer warrior and really inspired me to trust God with my life. She was the musical talent in the family. It came from my grandfather, her dad, Mr. Jim Leopold. I grew up singing in her church group.

My dad was a prince of a man. In a lot of movies about African American families the father is generally portrayed as a weak, unemployed, or having a problem with drugs, alcohol, or promiscuity. Not my dad! Every opportunity he had he told us how much he loved us. He would show me examples of other good men in the neighborhood and encouraged me to be like them. I truly admired my dad! He was a hard worker. Not only did he provide for his immediate family, but he literally took care of my mom's parents and her sister after her husband died. Even though our family consisted of seven children, anyone down on their luck could find a place to stay and a meal at our home. He did not attend church a lot because he was always at work however, I still saw more of God in him than in anyone who was in church every time the doors opened. I believe that though curses are generational, so are blessings! I have been blessed throughout my life because of my father's benevolence.

He was also a great storyteller. He should have been an author. He could tell the most spellbinding stories with side plots and he never lost his place in the story! On nights when there wasn't anything good on the radio, he would entertain us. My dad loved my mom dearly and treated my mom so well that her nick name was "Queenie!" I was always moved by the way he would never eat until all of us had eaten, children first.

I have lots of great memories of going fishing with Mom and my grandmother on the Mermentau River. I was able to play baseball and all kinds of games with my friends. I was even able to do some hunting for rabbits and blackbirds. It's amazing we all lived to be full grown adults because we would "kill 'em and eat 'em!" Whatever we killed we ate including armadillos and raccoons. It was an amazing time and I have no sad stories to tell.

Every summer I would move across the street to live with my maternal grandparents. They lived next to the church. My grandfather, Jim, had this incredible ability….I never saw him pick up a Bible, but he memorized verses. It was just unbelievable. He would tell you where the verse was and from which book in the Bible. He had failing eyesight so when the preachers would call out the Scripture, he would tell me where to find it.

I gave my heart to the Lord at an early age. I was around twelve years old and I remember sitting with my grandfather, Jim, listening to the preachers on the radio. At no point did anyone push me to accept Christ as my Savior, however, I was under such conviction just knowing that my life did not measure up to what I was reading to my grandfather and to what I was hearing on the radio, I just knew I needed Christ in my life. One Wednesday night they were having a business meeting at the church. I was under such conviction that I interrupted the meeting and asked them to pray for me. I received Him as my Savior that night. Unfortunately, there wasn't a youth group at our church, at least none my age, so I became a loner because I chose to follow Christ.

I formed my first singing group when I was nine or ten years old. We were called the "Riverside Five" because we were right by the Mermentau River. They were my classmates; Jessie Pattum, Jean Paul Taylor, and Lester and Chester O'Brian. Many groups would come through our town and sing at our church. They always came on a love offering basis. The group that came most often was the Midsouth Spiritual Singers. I don't think they were a great group artistically or musically, but they had such a wonderful spirit. The lead singer was Mr. Wilton Jones. He loved to sing and the fact that he would even embark on that kind of endeavor when there was no way they would make any money exemplified their love for Christ. They were an inspiration to me.

I sang in the church choir, but it wasn't really a choir, it was just a worship group that my mom put together. We were not polished, but we were anointed! My sisters, Marell and Margie (Nell) sang in the group along with my brother Calvin, my niece Dianna, and my other sister, Orelia plus a few members of the congregation. Marell was a great singer and a great communicator. When people saw us coming, they knew they were in for a good time because Marell could really bring it! I was the number two guy because I could make a gravelly sound like a Pentecostal preacher. It was remarkably similar, but not as excellent, as Teddy Pendergrass. That was considered special because I was only a teenager with that grown up sound. So, we were a great one, two punch! Of course, my mom was the leader of the group!

My brother, Jim, did not sing in the choir. He was an incredible singer and I always wanted to sing like him. I thought that I sounded like him when I would be doing all the tournaments at school and singing at different events. At that time Johnnie Mathis was popular and people would say, "You sound like Johnnie Mathis!" but I was trying to sound like James Barrett Andrus!

Andy, my oldest brother, had to change his name later in life. He was named Shirley because my mom wanted a girl. When he was in his 50's he changed his name officially to Andrew. He would not change his name until our mom passed away. We all called him Andy. Jim and Andy were all the things I was not. They were athletic, good looking and cool! They had charisma and everything. They were my heroes and I wanted to be just like them, but I never quite attained that. They were genuinely great guys and I miss them dearly.

As far back as I can remember my dream was to be a gospel singer. However, before I really zeroed in on Gospel music, I thought I was going to be a baseball player. I was a walking stat machine. I had stats on everybody. I knew the scores and I listened to the radio. Baseball was "King" back then and it was a national past time. I listened to the games every day and Jackie Robinson was my hero. He broke through the color barrier in baseball and his commitment always amazed me. Never in my wildest dreams did I imagine that I would be used in a similar fashion, not in sports, but in Gospel music. That's when I really got into baseball and I wanted to play. My brothers were excellent athletes, and I was "okay." I learned a lot from them as far as the game, but I did not have the natural talent they had. As a matter of fact, my first cousin, Earnest Leopold, we called him Gotch, was a much better athlete than I was. He was number 1 and I was number 2 and no one would let us play on the same team because together we were awesome. However, I couldn't touch him as far as his athletic ability was concerned. The other thing was…. I could really hit but I could not run. When you are a little guy and you run the hundred-yard dash in a day and a half, chances are you are not going to be a short stop in the major leagues, but I had a dream! I did play semi pro in college, but I was not good enough, so I turned all my attention to being a gospel singer.

At every opportunity I would tell my mom and dad about being a gospel singer. Late at night, lying across their bed with them, I would share my hopes and dreams with them. They really believed me. I think all my brothers and sisters also believed I would reach the goals I had set for myself because I was totally committed and driven. I won all kinds of awards in school. I belonged to a Pentecostal Christ Sanctified Holiness Church right across the street from my home. Going to church was not an elective at my home, especially for me. I had to be in church every time the door opened. You couldn't shy away from it because they would put the speakers in the windows so that you could hear them, and it was very boisterous! Because of the music and the loudness of the praise and worship, I couldn't fake it and say, "Oh, I didn't know that church was going on." The whole town knew it was going on!

School Days!

I was bussed to school from the 2nd grade through the 12th grade. I started singing in school when I was in elementary school. My first solo was *Pretend,* a song made famous by Nat King Cole. I had to sing it in front of the entire elementary school. I had to sing A cappella and I started it too high. I didn't do a particularly good job! I could hear people laughing and snickering in the audience. From that day forward I said, "They will never laugh at me again!" So, I redoubled my efforts to sing and to really become an accomplished singer. By the way, to add insult to injury, the white school was named Jennings High School and the black school was named Jefferson Davis High School….I could never wrap my head around that!

All through high school I started to get more attention from singing. In our school you competed and if you placed in the District competition with an Excellent or Superior you would go on the State Finals. Well, I would always compete in multiple areas like Civics, History and Current Events and would make it to the State Finals. I also went to State for music competition, usually in a group or as a soloist. I enjoyed school and when I started in high school, I had a teacher named Velta Shields. She had a great impact on my life. She somehow saw something in me that really piqued her interest because she invested a lot of time with me. To be very honest with you, the kids would tease me and call me "The Teacher's Pet!" Whenever I went to music class, I did not sit out in the class with the other kids, but I sat on the bench with her behind the piano. My voice was changing at that time, so she put me in the male quartet, and we went to the State finals with that group. I was the youngest in the group so the next year I started singing with a guy named Gene Davis. He was the brother of one my classmates, Johnnie Ray Davis, who is currently pastoring in Jennings, Louisiana. Gene was a great tenor! I was never really a tenor, but I could do all the falsetto and stuff. (I think I got all the falsetto and things from working with my mom's group in church.) As Mrs. Shields continued to work with me the following year, I did the tenor solo and went to the State finals at Southern University. As I said, I was not a real tenor, but I could do it….I could go in and out of falsetto and do it! The name of the song was "*When I've Sung My Songs to You*", and I knew I had won because when I came to the end of the song instead of singing a low note, I hit a high falsetto note and the judge dropped her pencil! She was impressed!

About this time people started coming to the school and inviting me to do various musical numbers at events around town. I don't know if they were talent scouting but there was always someone who was going to get me a record contract but that never happened! There were always black and white, mostly white adults who would come by and talk to me and after they would hear me sing, they would say, "Man, I can get you this, or I can get you that." Nothing ever happened.

So many teachers contributed to my life. Mrs. Velda Shields, my music teacher, Mrs. Juanita Thibideaux, Mrs. James Ward Jr. and others. The teachers, during that time, sacrificed a lot to help us in the black community. Our parents were illiterate or semi-illiterate and needed help in guiding us. I had teachers who would correct my grammar, because they said if you want to be a singer and travel all over the world, you need to speak correctly. They really came down hard on me as far as my diction! I worked extremely hard and they kept close eyes and ears on me. At that time, we did not have all the electives in school that students have now. We had reading, writing, and arithmetic. Our teachers were strong on that. They were very, very committed to us learning the basics.

Mrs. Velta Shields had a band from the high school, and I was the lead singer. They would do secular songs and my mom would let me sing them because I was doing it with the school. I always felt uncomfortable because I'd gathered from my experiences in church that if you sang anything that didn't have the "Big 3" in it, the Father, Son, and Holy Ghost, you were going straight to hell and you had backslidden. Singing with the high school band was my first time to sing non-gospel songs!

One year after our competition we had a talent show and I did Jerry Butler's, *For Your Precious Love* and everybody went crazy. I learned early on that I had a gift to mimic almost anyone's style of singing. Whoever had a hit I would sing it like they did! I sang that song just like Jerry Butler and I knew I had won but the judges would not give me 1st place. Instead, they called it a "tie" with the "hometown" guy from Baton Rouge, but everyone knew I had really been the winner. That talent contest put me in good standing with Southern University High School! I later received an invitation from them to be the guest artist at their prom. I had not planned on going to the prom because there was dancing and that was taboo in my church! However, since I was singing, my mom let me go. That opportunity gave me a lot of exposure to different people and ways of life. I made a lot of friends there, so I decided to go to Southern University. It was in the Southwest Athletic Conference, along with Grambling and Texas Southern. These are historically black Land Grant Colleges and were established in 1890.

During my first summer school session at Southern University, I won a talent show again.

I kind of got the "big head" because my very first week of school I'm getting to walk Miss Southern University to her dorm room, and I am a freshman! The Bible says in Proverbs 18:16, "A man's gift opens doors for him before great men." I believe that's what happened in my life. I became extremely popular in a short period of time. I don't say this in a braggadocious way, it's just that's the way it happened. I had never been in a place like that. I had come from a little town and then I was in a university with 5,000 students with more than half of them girls! I am just a little country boy. I was not promiscuous or anything like that, but I loved the attention the girls showed me because I was a singer. I was well known so ego got in the way. I still prayed and told people I was a Christian and I had certain standards, but the ego is a strange thing. As time passed, I became more and more popular. The band was a great professional band, and they invited me to be their lead singer. I tried to convince myself that I was singing their music to help my parents pay for my college education. I was only fooling myself.

I hung out with all the football and basketball players, even though I was just a freshman. Here again, "My gift madeth room for me." My first girlfriend was a junior and every couple of weeks I had a different girlfriend because I had never seen so many girls in my life.

As I mentioned earlier, segregation was a very real thing in Louisiana. The law in Louisiana said that if you had 1/32 of black blood in your ancestry, you were considered black. You were required to go to a segregated public school, (1st grade-12th) and could not go to school with whites. In Louisiana this included colleges as well. During that time, I went to school with students who were white, but somewhere in their background they had some black blood in them. One of my great friends, Bill Hydell, was like that. He came from a well-to-do family. He had fiery red hair and freckles. You would have thought he was Caucasian until he opened his mouth! He was loud and wrong and strong! We had a great friendship and stayed friends through college. I have lost track of him, but he was a great guy, and we had a lot of fun together. Before James Brown put out the song, *I'm Black and I'm Proud*, the lighter complexion students would stay to themselves. They would not mingle with the darker complexion students; they were cordial but did not want to mix blood. They wanted to keep the purity of their lightness. Hydell was not like that at all. He was simply crazy. He had a sister and they invited me to their home. You didn't need to worry about her though, she had nothing to do with me…she was cool to me and that's how it was back then. That was before Black was beautiful. One of the things that really plagued me was growing up in segregation. You were demeaned and made to feel worthless by such signs as, "White's Only", "Colored Water Fountain", and being guilty until proven innocent. There were many things I loved about Louisiana, like the food and the people, but I knew I did not want to live there. There were very few good opportunities to excel for blacks in the area where I lived. I actually thought that someone from the established church would speak out about segregation, but the silence was deafening. That hurt me a great deal and I could never reconcile being a Christian and not loving everyone and being equal. So consequently, I was confused about my walk with God. I felt the church, not God, had let me down. The only reason I was able to achieve, grow, and have ambition was because of the love of my parents. They helped restore my sense of personal worth.

I was taught so much in church about fire and brimstone and that's it's better to marry than to burn! I wanted to marry early because I couldn't handle all my emotions. I wanted to live for God and the only way I thought I could live a successful Christian life was to be married. It wasn't that I was promiscuous, it's just that I had never been in such tempting situations before. I especially felt that way after I met a young lady named Delores Ricard. She was beautiful. I was doing a show with the band when she walked in. Our eyes met and boy that was it. She was from a small town, Amite, Louisiana. On our campus you could find whatever you wanted as far as color and characteristics. She was much lighter than I, and had green eyes, but she was not into her color. She was just a nice person and we became close, almost inseparable.

It's hard to explain, but I was under so much conviction by the Holy Ghost that I was terribly unhappy. I started to get physically ill because I was not using my voice for what God had intended. I got so ill I called my mom, and they came to take me home from Baton Rouge. They took me to church and an evangelist, Aunt Ola, prayed for me, along with the rest of the church. Just like that the spirit of depression left!

My mom was smart, and she knew that Delores had really impacted my life so when I came back home a few weeks later, she sent me to California to live with my brother, Jim. That move woke me up about my relationship with my Delores. Later, I will share with you how we reconnected fifty years later, and it was like finding a long lost relative.

In 1964 my friend, Bernie Adams and I joined the National Guard. A lot of people were able to get out of military service because they claimed to be conscientious objectors. I couldn't say that because I was not one! Bernie looked at me one day and said, "We'd better join the National Guard, or they are going to send us to Viet Nam." So, we joined!

We were sent to Fort Ord in Northern California and took our basic training together. I was in superb shape when I went into the military because I had been lifting weights and working out. Other men were not as ready! I had been in ROTC and so was made a squad leader. Bernie had more college experience in ROTC and was made a platoon leader. These assignments gave us perks like a private room and a position of authority. I have Bernard to thank for that experience and we were in active duty for eight months. After six weeks we graduated from basic training and my MOS school for training for office work as a clerk. I enjoyed my time in the military although I was frustrated all the time because I did not enjoy being told what to do! I was a free spirit and had spent most of my time around the church and was not used to all the foul language and the harassment of the recruits. I probably weighed 155lbs. at that time because I was more muscular.

Every day we had the "daily dozen' exercises and I expected it to be easy, but their intent was to break you down physically and break your spirit. For the next six years I had to attend one weekend a month and two weeks each summer on active duty. I'm glad I went into the military because I was somewhat sheltered around that time. Due to my upbringing in Louisiana, I had not had the opportunity to interact with people who were different than I. It was quite a challenge to keep my position as squad leader for the entire basic training. Many people started as squad leaders and were demoted. I came close a couple of times, but I made it! I think my success was fueled by my anger at not wanting to be there and I did not like seeing the way other people were treated by the drill sergeants. There were only a few black men in the National Guard in my company and the sergeants seemed to be intent on making life miserable for everyone. Many of the recruits were cussed out and treated badly and that did not set well with me. The mistreatment of others has always bothered me, and I wanted no part of it.

It seemed that people were afraid of me because you are never supposed to volunteer for anything in the Army. The drill sergeant would ask for volunteers for hand-to-hand combat. I volunteered even though you were used as a rag doll to throw around and to demonstrate different fighting techniques. It didn't hurt me because I was in great shape. When we had drills within the platoon you had to match up with someone and I was always outweighed by 30 lbs. People thought I was the bravest guy they had ever seen, and no one wanted to mess with me. Many of the men were older than I and the National Guard was full of draft dodgers. At that time, the recruits were mistreated physically, and no one cared! One of the tests included running a mile with all your gear in a specific time. If you failed, you had to take basic training all over again. I had shin splints but passed the test! Once you made it through basic training, it was great. At the time of the Los Angeles Watts riots, our entire company, along with others, were told that we were going to have to take riot training. The commanding officer who was doing the training said, "If you see a rioter running with a television, don't shoot because you might hit the tv". I got up and walked out. My commander told me that if I did not take the training, I would be up for a court martial. I told them I needed to make a phone call and I called Winnie, and said, "You aren't going to see me for a while because I am going to be court martialed." I then said, I need to make one more call, to the Times to share my story. All at once it seemed like a light came on with them, and they told me I did not have to take the training. I then partnered up with another guy, Neuby, and he was the meanest guy in the Guard. He was a staunch militant and believed in Mao Tse-Tung. He and I sat in the jeep together. He read The Red Book while I was reading the Bible. No one messed with us.

During basic training, the supply sergeant invited me to a church in Seaside, California. Very few men in the Guard went to church but he and I had developed a common bond through Christ. I was so happy to be in church and it became my salvation.

Interestingly enough, I also made some extra money by loaning others money for all their bad habits. When I came home from my basic training, I found that Andrae had left a message with my sister and he wanted me to join him in The Disciples. My life was about to change!

Winnie Holman Andrus

Winnie, the Love of My Life!

In 1965 Winnie Holman, her sister, Shirley, and her mother, Emma, moved to Los Angeles, California. They were trying to find a place to live and ended up staying with a distant cousin of mine, and their uncle by marriage, Simon Guidry. Simon and his wife, Lydia, made them feel right at home in California and one night Simon called me on the phone and said, "Sherman, I want you to meet two girls from San Augustine, Texas before the wolves get to them!" I was not interested in meeting any girls from Texas, but they invited me to dinner. I really didn't want to go so I was late getting there. It was awful! I met Shirley, and she was cute, but when I met Winnie, she was a knock-out, absolutely stunning! The minute she turned the corner in the house, I said to myself, "I'm going to marry that girl!" She was so articulate, and I had always wanted a girl who was articulate because always in my mind, I saw myself being in front of people and needing someone who was comfortable with people. I knew I needed someone who would be able to express themselves and Winnie was perfect!

Of course, you know I have this weird sense of humor, so when she said she was from Texas, I said, "Oh, I can tell you are from Texas because I can still see the mud on your ankles!" Honestly, I have no idea where that came from and if I could have cut my tongue out, I would have! What a dumb thing to say! The amazing thing is that she still was willing to talk to me and as we got to know each other better, we really liked each other. I don't think she was attracted to me, but I was totally attracted to her. She had a boyfriend back home that she thought she was going to marry so she didn't really connect with me like I connected with her, but she said she thought it would be fun to go out with a nice guy. We began to talk all the time and to do things together. That night, after I met her, I called my friend, Bernard, and said, "Hey! I just met the girl I am going to marry!" About a year and half later, on June 18, 1966, I married her. Andrae's father performed the ceremony and Andrae, Perry and Fredrick Bean were all in our wedding. Bernard Adams was my best man. Winnie has been my partner in life for more than 54 years. She supported me when we moved from her beloved California to Nashville, from Nashville to Oklahoma, from Oklahoma to Hawaii, from Hawaii back to Oklahoma and all the places in between. She has attended a multitude of concerts and was always loving and kind to the fans who loved meeting her. She supported me as I transitioned from The Disciples to The Imperials, to Andrus, Blackwood, and Company and to Andrus and Bingle. Many of her friends did not believe in my ministry because they had never seen anyone in the black community in full-time ministry as a singer, and not be a minister. They did not understand the life we had with the popularity and the style of living we shared because it was not a usual thing in our community. She never faltered in her belief of me and my dreams for ministry. She helped with the record table or wherever she was needed. Winnie is fiercely independent and always had her own life as did Sherman Jr. I was gone a lot, but God blessed us with a strong marriage that has withstood many battles and struggles. She always worried about me on the road; was I eating right, getting enough sleep, working too hard and so on. We are still happily married and looking forward to celebrating our 55th wedding anniversary! She is the love of my life! Wow! It has been a great journey, but she has made it even better!

Winnie and Sherman Andrus at the Grammy Awards.

Winnie Holman Andrus and Sister, Shirley Holman Porter

Our Son, Sherman Jr.

On June 8, 1969, Winnie gave birth to a beautiful baby boy, Sherman Jr. and our lives were forever changed! He was a very quick bright baby and easy to care for. He and his mom would drive cross-country from Nashville to Las Vegas. He learned to read by reading billboards. He was extremely intelligent, looked like Winnie, and had my personality. He and Winnie were very much alike. They loved food and were very particular. One of my memories was when they ordered room service at a hotel while I was singing at Southern Methodist University. They spent over $100.00 and they had side orders of hamburgers! I never was invited to return!

Sherman Jr. started school in Madison, TN. The teachers knew of The Imperials, so subsequently they knew me. He was an avid reader and the teacher contacted us and had us provide special books to challenge his reading. He started the second grade in Oklahoma City in the Putnam City School District. He was so excited because he was in accelerated learning classes, much like Gifted and Talented and absolutely loved it! As a high school graduate, he was a National Merit Scholar. I was privileged to speak at his high school baccalaureate service. I actually got him in trouble because I joked about the fact that there were students with a four-point grade average who wore gold robes and Sherman had told me they had simply paid more for them! . He could have gone to any of the regional schools free, but he wanted to go to California to Pepperdine University. I had a long talk with him about how life was going to be different in California. At Putnam City High School, he had grown up with a predominately white group of students, who simply saw him as Sherman. I wanted him to know that at Pepperdine, people were going to see his color. He didn't believe me at first but when he came home the first time, he told me I was right. There is systemic racism in some places. It is so strange that you must prepare your children for that kind of thinking. He was not going to just be accepted as he had been but would have to prove himself and deal with prejudice.

Coincidentally, at one time I was going to fly to California and drive straight back from Pepperdine with Sherman at a semester break. I had been singing at Dallas, TX and caught the plane to fly to California. I had been flying so much that I was "platinum" on American Air lines (I have flown over 1 million miles on American!) and they allowed me to board the airplane first in the first-class section. I was unaware that Michael Jackson and his entire entourage were already on board. There was one seat left in first class and they gave it to me. It just so happened I was sitting next to Seth Riggs, a voice coach-instructor to the stars, and he had come on the road to help Michael because the songs were so high. We were having a great conversation and Michael came up and introduced himself to me, of course he needed no introduction! He offered some gum to Seth because he said he knew his breath was killing me! I told him that I knew he wouldn't remember me but that I had met him and a couple of his brothers at Vee Jay Recording Studios when I was with Andrae. Of course, he didn't remember me but as a side note, Vee Jay Records was the record label who brought the Beatles over to the U.S. It had been primarily a black artist's recording label prior to that time. The Capitol recording label took over the Beatles' contract later. I was able to get Michael Jackson's autograph for Sherman Jr. as Sherman was 18 years old at that time.

He met and married Mary Yacob in 1991, during his last year at Pepperdine. Mary is bi-racial, and he was being hassled frequently by police when they were together. Although she was Ethiopian and Irish, she did not look Ethiopian, but she looked more like she was Hispanic. One day he called me and asked if I could help him move to the Washington D.C. area because it was more progressive. I told him I would try, so I called Mark Pickens, my friend and owner of Armstrong United Van Lines, to see if he could move him. He moved Sherman Jr., lock, stock, and barrel to Germantown, Md. When Sherman asked him how much he owed, he said, "I can't charge you anything because your dad is one of my best friends." Over the years, Mark and his wife, Lauren, have been extremely supportive of my ministry.

Sherman Jr. and Mary had two beautiful children, Patrick, and Samantha. They moved from Germantown, MD to Portland, Oregon and built their life there. At one time while Sherman was working for INTEL, he headed up a division of a company in Kuala Lumpur in Malaysia. Mary and the children were able to visit him while he was there which was quite an experience for them. Sherman, like Winnie, loved Hawaii and he took the family there often. His favorite island was the Big Island! In 2013 he was diagnosed with lung cancer and passed away a year later. The worst day of my life was when I walked into his hospital room and he was lying lifeless on the bed. He wasn't even covered. Winnie looked at me and asked, "Isn't there something you can do?" I felt absolutely helpless. That moment still haunts me to this day.

We miss him terribly because we often laughed about things that we saw differently than others. He was a great help to me with the computer and technology and he kept me abreast of things on the internet. He would always let me know what people were saying about me on sites like Facebook and was proud to see his name and mine. I think his untimely death affected Winnie to the degree that it exacerbated her illness and subsequently led to her move to a nursing home. I truly regret, and have great pain, that our grandchildren are not a part of our lives and neither is their mother.

Sherman Andrus Sr., Sherman Andrus Jr. & Winnie Andrus, 2010

Winnie Andrus, Sherman Andrus Sr. & Sherman Jr. 1976

California Connections

I n California in 1963, I joined Grace Memorial Church of God in Christ. My home church in Louisiana was Pentecostal but not a part of the Church of God in Christ. It was a large church and I attended but did not really know anyone there. One afternoon at a service I met Gloria Jones, lead singer for Andrae Crouch's group, "The COGICS" and through her I met Andrae. I started attending her church. It was much smaller, and I started singing in their choir. Gloria Jones' father was a famous evangelist in the Church of God in Christ. He was called Baby Jones. I think his mantle of anointing fell on Gloria for she was an anointed singer, and I was in love with her voice! At one of our services Andrae heard me sing and he told me that if he ever started a male group, he wanted me to sing with him. The members of the "COGICS" were Andrae's sister, Sandra, Billy Preston who played the organ and sang, Gloria Jones, Sandra Williams, Edna Wright, and Frankie Springs.

During that time, every Sunday afternoon, we would have concerts. We would have a variety of groups from the Southern California area. Some of them went on to great careers in rock and popular music. Mary Clayton was a great singer! She went on to do recording sessions with several artists including a duet with Mick Jagger, *Gimme Shelter*. She was in a major accident and had to have both legs amputated. I don't remember her as Mary Clayton, but as "Baby Sister", which is what we called her. Thelma Houston was a member of the Art Reynolds Singers. They were the first group to record, *Jesus Is Just Alright*! Thelma is best known for her mega hit, *Don't Leave Me This Way*. That was before the Doobie Brothers. Mel Carter was another great singer, and Lou Rawls, who appeared with the Pilgrim Travelers, was their lead singer. It was at one of these concerts I first heard Andrae Crouch's big hit, *The Blood Will Never Lose Its Power*.

Bili Thedford, (Aka Billi Red), Sherman Andrus Sr., Ruben
Fernandez, Perry Morgan, & Andrae Crouch

Life with Andrae Crouch

Andrae was my mentor. Even though we were the same age, he had much more worldly experience than I. His dad was a minister and a bishop in the Church of God in Christ. He had lots of exposure and everyone knew him, and he knew everybody. To this day I am thankful that I met him for he certainly assisted me in achieving my dreams to sing for the Lord. I have been doing that for over fifty years and my professional career began with Andrae Crouch and The Disciples. I was working at the post office as a temporary clerk and was able to take off without pay and keep my job. Andrae was working at David Wilkerson's Teen Challenge and was in charge of the Addicts Choir or Ex Addicts Choir and I would go and help him. He would have me sing with the choir and we traveled all over Southern California. Andrae was a musical genius, yet he really took me under his wing and I so appreciate everything he did for me.

At that time Pastor David Wilkerson wrote a book, The Cross and The Switchblade about his ministry with gangs in New York and his spiritual mentoring of Niki Cruz. He started out in New York but would come to Melody Land Christian Center once a month to host big rallies. He had a strong impact on my life! We would come to sing with the choir and David Wilkerson was a strait-laced guy. When he first started, if you wore a colored shirt with a tie, he felt that was just too much. Our music was kind of different, but we were always there as his guests. He would pack the place out every month. It was a theater in the round, and he would preach but he preached the same sermon every time! It was so amazing! At the close of each sermon he would say, "I am coming to a close now and I want you to think about responding to what God is saying to you." People would just begin to come to the front from all over the auditorium. I was so amazed because it let me know, "not by power nor by might but by His Spirit." This man was truly anointed of God. I genuinely believe that God gave him prophetic words. It is alleged that in 1986 he shared with a friend, Mike Evans, that a global pandemic was coming. It could very well be that the COVID-19 pandemic we are having right now was prophesied by him in 1986.

David really loved the song, *Without A Song* and it was powerful. Whenever we sang that song, we brought the house down! We loved it so much it was on *Take the Message Everywhere*, our first album, God was really blessing me, and I was so thankful. I had turned my life around from the little time I was in college and I knew that God had given me a dream and an amazing opportunity to sing for Him. He also loved the song, *"I've Got Confidence"* and was featured in the movie, The Cross and The Switchblade." At that time Dave Wilkerson was looking for a singer and he invited me to travel with him as his featured soloist. Andrae and I talked it over and I decided it was best for me to stay with Andrae. He was my mentor, I was newly married, and I was happy with the choice I felt God was leading me to make. Dallas Holm became the lead soloist for Dave Wilkerson, and he was a great fit for that ministry. You see I believe that everything is ordered by God. The Bible tells us that the steps of the righteous man are ordered by God. I had no problem with that! I felt like God is going to do what God is going to do. My grandfather used to say, "He is God all by himself, He don't need nobody else."

As Andrae and I worked more together, he would have me sing most of the ballads while he did the hard stuff, hard gospel. I was blessed because he really trained me well. I want to give him credit for helping a lot of singers get their start through gospel music. At that time particularly, there were lots of gospel singers in Los Angeles. There were many talented people but what made the difference was the anointing of God. I believe more than anything else that I have a gift from God and have been anointed to do what I have done. There were a lot of musical people on my mom's side, but I do believe that the anointing that was on my great grandfather to my grandfather, fell on me! I had an incredible time singing with Andrae and it buoyed my hopes and dreams to know that people cared so much about me. We had a wonderful rapport with the young people at that time, and they loved me very much! We would travel to places all over Southern California, especially Youth for Christ rallies, and had a great time with all the youth that attended!

We were blessed to work with Ken Overstreet at that time and he had the biggest chapter of Youth for Christ in the San Diego area. We would go sing at Balboa Park and pack the place out! The kids treated us like rock stars! They loved us and would scream, and clap and just enjoy our music! What is so amazing is that this was predominately a white audience. We rarely sang to a black audience. We were blessed to be one of most popular groups on the West Coast of California at that time. Andrae was writing songs and teaching them to me. Things were snowballing for us and out of the blue we were contacted by Dr. John Haggai. He saw our album, *Take the Message* Everywhere, in a UniMart store. Many of you reading this may not know what an album is. At that time, we recorded music on 12-inch vinyl discs, and they were sold in stores. Dr. Haggai got in touch with Andrae and we were able to go full time in sharing the gospel through music.

As I reflect on my journey, I realize that the days with Andrae Crouch and The Disciples were some of the most exciting days of my ministry. We were all so young and innocent, and tender to the things of God. We didn't want to do anything that would prohibit us or stall us in our decision to live for God and to be used by Him. We were really on fire for the Lord and we experienced a miracle almost every week! We were all working regular jobs, five days a week, and then we had opportunities every weekend to minister. We did have a few concerts during the week but mostly Friday through Sunday. As I mentioned earlier, I was working at the Post Office and I took a shift that started at 4:15 in the morning till 12:45 in the afternoon. That enabled me to be free to go and do things with Andrae at Teen Challenge.

Our adventure was just beginning, and it started to really take off! Two of the other guys could not travel full-time because they were working, so our very first gig was just Andrae and me! We went to Seattle and did a guest concert called, *Sonata In Soul*, at Seattle Pacific College which is now Seattle Pacific University. We did very well and sold out of our 45 extended play record which included songs like *"Come and Go with Me to My Father's House"*, and *"Prayer is the Key to Heaven!"* We also received a great honorarium! They loved us so much that it gave us confidence that we could do more. In the Seattle area we stayed with some great people, Dorrie and Warren Gifford. They were incredible people. They did not have any children, so they were like mommy and daddy to us. Andrae had met them when he first took the Teen Challenge Addict Choir, then later they adopted me too. Their home church, Christian Temple, was a large congregation and their pastors were Ralph and Delores Sanders. We became friends with Ralph and Delores and their congregation. They just poured love into us. Their church served as our headquarters. We were unaware that Gospel Music had a circuit for gospel groups, we just trusted God and He opened doors. We were driving a Ford Econoline van sleeping on seats while others were traveling on buses, but we had an anointing of the Holy Spirit on our lives and on our music. We never felt any pressure, we simply went on stage and the Holy Spirit moved in a mighty way. I wouldn't have cared if we were on stage with Stevie Wonder, the Beatles, or the Jackson Five, nothing could compare or take the place of serving with Andrae under the anointing of the Spirit of God!

Andrae was the most anointed person I had ever been around. I grew up in a small church that was an off shoot of the Church of Christ. It wasn't a part of the Church of God in Christ denomination but was known as the Christ Sanctified Holiness Church. There were lots of differences due to regional behaviors. To quote some of the people, "If you live in a state where tobacco is being grown, then it is ok to smoke because smoking is not that bad, it's just a habit. People would say it was a bad habit, a filth to your body, but not a sin." That was the belief in the

Christ Sanctified Holiness Church. Smoking was accepted by them along with the Missionary Baptist and Southern Baptist churches. Many times, you would see people huddled outside the church smoking before and after service. My parents smoked but none of the kids did. We grew up in a home where they did not go outside to smoke. It was a daily ritual with my parents. I am blessed to still be here because of all my exposure to second hand smoke!

Getting back to Andrae! Andrae's dad prayed for him that he would have the gift because he needed a musician. I am telling you that Andrae was gifted! He could read chords, but he never really read music in the true sense of the word. He was a musical genius. I don't believe that the great pianist, Erroll Garner, ever read music but he was a genius and that's where Andrae was as well. With background vocals, he just had it! He would come up with arrangements and we would sing them. I was blessed to have his friendship! He and Winnie really got along well. He loved Winnie and she loved him. He was more worried about Winnie when she was pregnant than I was! He wanted to be sure that everything was ok for the baby boy that was coming into our lives.

A little later Andrae and I went to Hawaii. That was quite a trip! Andrae was handling all the details and he was not a detail person. Andrae was a brilliant musician and he always moved by faith and God always made a way. When we arrived at the airport the pastor who had invited us said, "You guys know where you are staying?' We thought he was taking care of everything, but we had nothing in writing. Andrae looked at me and I looked at him. I had some money because I had been married only a short time and Winnie was working. She had helped us save some money; it was enough for the hotel! Someone secured island rates for us, extremely reasonable, but we didn't have a lot of money! While we were there, we met a lady who was strong in the Assembly of God church. Her name was Florence Iszumi, and her husband was a police captain. She owned apartment buildings and she put us up in one of her apartments, free of charge. We did concerts at all the churches and they loved us! The Izumis were special friends. Sadly, she and her husband passed away in the last ten years. They became a part of our family, in fact, Winnie, Sherman Jr. and I spent Thanksgiving with them. They were wonderful people and I thank God for them and what a witness they were to us.

During our whole time in Hawaii, we could see God miraculously opening doors for us! The best part of working with Andrae Crouch and The Disciples was letting God provide as none of us had experience yet in the business aspect of our ministry. God always provided through his people.

Looking back at my life, I have been blessed to be with The Imperials, Andrus, Blackwood, & Co., and Andrus and Bingle, but traveling with Andrae and The Disciples has been the highlight of my life because of the miracles I saw each day.

Andrae Crouch and The Disciples

The members of Andrae Crouch and The Disciples were Bili Thedford, Perry Morgan, Sherman Andrus Sr., and Andrae Crouch. On our first album, *Take The Message Everywhere*, we had a Hispanic brother, Ruben Fernandez, join us. He was a great guy and was a close friend of Andrae's. Andrae thought that having Ruben in the group would really help him in his walk with God. I'm sure it did because he was a fabulous guy to be around. We became friends and enjoyed working together. We were very blessed that we did not have any problems in our group. Another exciting time for me was when Andrae produced my first solo album, *I've Got Confidence*. Andrae wrote eight songs for that album. *I've Got Confidence* he wrote especially for me as a motto for me because of my confidence in God and his direction for my life. The Benson Company would like to have signed Andrae Crouch and The Disciples on their label, but they were already on the Light Label of Word Records. Bob McKenzie, the producer from the Benson label, saw me in concert with the group and was amazed at the response I got from the kids, so he offered to do my solo album with Benson on the IMPACT label. They believed I was up and coming and that my association with Andrae would help with the record sales. I believe that Bob McKenzie was instrumental in my becoming an Imperial. He told them about me and my interaction with the audience and their response to me. I was not under any illusions about my role, I was just excited to get the album done!

Bili and Perry were wonderful men, much taller than I, but great to work with. Bili was about 6'3" and Perry was around 6'2". They were handsome men and great friends. I was always treated like a little brother, even though I was quite a bit older than Perry. Bili and I were close to the same age, yet they welcomed me into the group even though I was the last to join. They could have made my life miserable, but they didn't! They understood that Andrae wanted me to be the lead singer and there was never any question about that at all. No one begrudged Andrae's decision. While with the group, Columbia Records, offered me a solo record contract. I would be doing music like Johnny Mathis, but I was very conflicted from my time of singing secular songs with the band when I was in college. Andrae encouraged me to stay with the group and I did. I believe it was the right thing to do….God's ways are perfect!

Andrae Crouch and The Disciples: First World Tour

Around 1968, the Lord brought Ralph Carmichael, the great Christian composer and conductor, into our lives. Mr. Carmichael was an arranger of both secular pop music and contemporary Christian music. He became Nat King Cole's regular arranger and arranged music for other great artists such as Ella Fitzgerald, Peggy Lee, Bing Crosby, and many others. He also did music scores for albums and movies, including "The Cross and the Switchblade." He founded Light Records for Christian artists and after hearing some of Andrae's songs, he put Andrae Crouch and The Disciples on Light Records. Light Records is a subsidiary of WORD Records and our first album, *Take the Message Everywhere,* was produced, That album was truly a miracle because most groups had to scratch and try to find money to do an album but ours was paid for by Light Records. It did very well for us and put us on the map for Contemporary Christian music. We had one miracle right after another! We were able to go full-time and Dr. John Haggai, a minister from Atlanta, GA, invited us to go on a semi-world tour with him. We had to raise our own support, so we hosted a big concert at the Embassy Auditorium in Los Angeles, CA. All our friends and associates in other gospel groups participated in the concert to provide for our salaries for the tour. Some of the groups were The Accents with Rusty Peavy, Dave Peterson and Eddie Chavis; Gary Archer, older brother of The Archers, and The Noblemen which included Bill Murray, The Velvetones, Charles McPheeters and Children of The Day and others.

Dr. Haggai paid all our expenses. Our trip was a turning point in my life. I had always seen myself, in my mind's eye, ministering all over the world and God brought it to pass miraculously! We flew from Los Angeles to Tokyo to Jakarta, Indonesia. That was my first long trip out of the country. From Indonesia we went to Vietnam and entertained our US troops.

From there we went to Thailand and then back to England, Ireland, and Scotland. We had great meetings and it underscored our calling and reassured us that God had His Hand on our lives. We did not know anything about promoting ourselves, but God just took control and worked miracles in our lives. I had no idea how God was going to open doors for me through this experience. I have done a lot of great things since then but the initial thing, knowing that God's Hand is on you and He is going to take care of you, was a lesson I have never forgotten. I am so thankful for all that He has done for us!

One of the highlights while we were in Indonesia was meeting a popular singer named Henny Porwonogora. She was singing at the International Hotel in the big restaurant there. She was considered the number one pop singer in Indonesia. In the evenings we would go there to eat and just sit and listen to her. She was absolutely beautiful, young, and beautiful, and could sing on top of all of that! She would sing American songs and for some reason, she and I became friends. Andrae talked me into doing a duet with her and we sang "*Let It Be Me*". We had a great response from the audience and after that we became great friends. She was younger than I and just incredible. When she went out, she always traveled with bodyguards because her fans would mob her. She was a very playful young lady, like a child in many ways, and extremely popular. Some of the members of Dr. Haggai's staff saw her and asked me to talk with her and to gain her confidence. One evening I shared Christ with her, and she gave her heart to the Lord. We invited her to come to our concerts and she did! We were in an auditorium that held about 15,000 and we were drawing about 8,000 people but when she would come, we would have standing room only! She didn't sing, but simply sat on the stage with us and that was all that was needed. Her presence helped put us over the top with the Indonesians. We often took train trips to the outlying areas away from Jakarta and she would go with us, along with her mom and her bodyguards. We had a great friendship. Dr. Haggai's staff became jealous of our relationship and talked to Andrae about it. They told him it didn't look good even though her mother and her bodyguards were always with her . I was black and she was Asian---they found fault with me because of racial prejudice. They gave me a foretaste of what was I was going to encounter as I broke the color barrier and entered Southern Gospel Music. I don't know where she is now. I saw some pictures of her on the internet, but I wish I could let her know that she was a great help to us at that time. When I went home, she sent all kind of things to my home in California for Winnie. She sent exotic materials and cloth to make dresses and clothing. Her friendship gave us the "Stamp of Approval" we needed in Indonesia. It is amazing how God puts the right people in our lives at just the time we need them most.

When we returned from Indonesia, Andrae became extremely sick. We had booked a tour through Texas with one stop being at Baylor University in Waco and Andrae was unable to go. Our group was so new that when I took over as the lead for the group, no one knew the difference and Danny Lee came along as our accompanist. Leading the group gave me great confidence in being able to lead the group on the stage and be a soloist on stage. I loved being the emcee and interacting with the crowd. This became my strong suit when I joined The Imperials.

This tour was just the beginning of an amazing journey for me! Our popularity was spreading like wildfire! It's strange but when God begins to open doors for you and to do things for you, you meet a lot of people who don't necessarily have your best interests at heart. They see a chance to take advantage of you. We had several people that Andrae met who would try to convince him to do our music in a different way. We were a predominately black group with one Hispanic member, Ruben Fernandez, and our audiences were predominately white and Hispanic. Unfortunately, at that time, our music never caught on with the Church of God in Christ people. Later, Andrae became more vested in black gospel and his popularity increased. When I left, Tremaine Hawkins worked with the group temporarily as did Danny Bell Hall and Tata Vega, Linda McCrary, Kristle Murden. A group out of New York, called Sweet Spirit, worked with Andrae as well. It's hard for me to say, but tongue in cheek, "I think I was holding Andrae back!" He really flourished!

When we completed the tour, we took some time off and took our wives and families to Hawaii. We had a great time there. We stayed at this quaint hotel right on the beach, the Surf Rider Moana. It did not have any air conditioning but had ceiling fans and we thought that was very romantic! It was very inexpensive at that time but since has become one of the most expensive hotels in Hawaii. God just blessed our families, and we were so grateful!

May 1, 1969 was a pivotal day in my life. We were going back to Seattle with the group and were looking forward to being there because the kids loved us! I was sitting at a red light in a Volkswagen bug, thinking about the trip to Seattle and excited that as soon as my day was over, I would be with the group to sing. In those days we did not fly but rather we had an old Ford customized van with seats to ride in or you could sleep on the floor! Since it was just the four of us it didn't really matter. However, on this trip we were going to fly so I was looking forward to the trip. From the time I stopped at the red light until I woke up on a stretcher in an ambulance, I have no memory of what happened. I woke up and the EMS driver asked me if I was ok and I said "Yes, I have this trip and I am going to Seattle." They said that maybe I needed to think about it for a while. I then learned that I had a concussion and there would be no trip for me that day! They took me to the hospital, but the hospital did not admit me and when Winnie came to pick me up, I was standing on the corner. I didn't even know where I was because no one wheeled me out or had me wait in the lobby. I was still dazed! I won't give you the name of the hospital because I do not want to be sued!

Now you must understand that Winnie was eight months pregnant at the time with Sherman Jr. He was born on June 8, 1969, a little over a month later! When Winnie was pregnant, she was absolutely beautiful! Many women gain a lot of weight when they are pregnant, but Winnie was just the opposite! I don't believe she has ever been that slender in her life! She took me home to our apartment and my sisters and brothers came to see me, but I had no idea where I was. I later learned that while I was sitting at the red light I was hit by a drunk driver. Thankfully, I had no serious injuries, just bruises and a concussion. It is amazing how God can bring good out of bad things that happen in our lives. I had no idea I was so loved by the people who followed our group, but Andrae brought back bags of get-well cards from all these kids who loved us! It was really something and it touched my heart! I knew that God had called me to do this since I was a little boy, and those kids with their cards, underscored the fact that this was my calling! Please understand this is not hero worship, but rather it is a love that God puts in the hearts of His people. They want to nurture and support you because of the gift that God has given you. It is not an ego thing nor is it about your talent, but it is about how committed you are to God and how the Holy Spirit works through you!

The Southern Gospel scene was much different than the gospel concerts on the west coast. The Disciples had to be incredibly careful about how we approached the ladies in our audience. Because we were an all-black group, singing to a predominately white audience, we were especially careful not to offend anyone. At Southern Gospel concerts there was a lot more physical interaction with the audience than what we experienced on the coast. At the "All Night Sings" a popular song like *Touring That City* or *I Know, I Know* would be sung by every group that appeared on the stage that night. Each group felt like their particular rendition was best. It was entertainment! At that time, The Imperials were the "gold standard." They were not great performers, simply great singers. The Oak Ridge Boys were always a difficult group to follow because they were good performers! When I later joined The Imperials, it took me quite a while to get used to the different climate at the concerts.

The Brethren- Ike Jones(Deceased), Sherman Andrus Sr., David Botello,
Marvin Steelman, Carlos Ramos, & Danny Diangelo(Deceased)

Transitioning from The Disciples

When I left Andrae and The Disciples, there was no conflict, but the Lord was dealing with me and confirmed that my calling was to be a solo artist and merely work on weekends. I had gone back to a regular job and was excited to be a soloist. The booking agent that had booked The Disciples, approached me, and suggested that I could get more bookings if I had a group. Danny Angelo, of The Disciples, contacted me and said he was available and that he had some friends who would love to be a part of the music group. They were all from the San Francisco area. We added a studio pianist, Ike Jones, and formed The Brethren. David Botello played guitar, Carlos Ramos played the bass, and our sound man was Marvin Steelman. My case had not been settled yet on the accident caused by the drunk driver, so my lawyer advanced money to me. With that money I bought a sound system and an old school bus. We were off and running! It was quite simple. The name of our booking agency was Van Woodward Associates, who also booked Larry Norman, and we looked for opportunities to minister. Just as we were about to break even, the guys from San Francisco wanted to go back home because they missed their girlfriends. The group disbanded after six months.

With tears streaming down my face, I walked into our apartment. I remember this so vividly! I walked into our bedroom in our apartment crying and Winnie asked me, "Why are you crying?" I didn't even realize I was crying! I told her "The guys don't want to be in the group anymore, but it doesn't bother me!" Winnie knew I was hurting deep inside and she just held me and told me it was going to be all right. Then to add insult to injury, Marvin Steelman had our bus because he was our driver and our sound man. I told him I needed to return the bus so that I would be free from anymore expenses. He told me I could not have the bus until I gave him the $200.00 that he gave the group. His gift was unsolicited, but he wanted it back. I then did something that even bothers me to this day. I have always helped my parents and never asked them for anything. With tears again streaming down my face, I asked my parents to send me $200.00 so I could pay Marvin. They sent it and I was so thankful and have paid them back many times over!

With no group to be concerned about I had a lot of free time! Jimmy and Carol Owens invited me to sing in their musical, *Show Me*, as lead singer. Jamie Owens Collins, Randy Stonehill, and Michael O'Martian were also in the show. Michael O'Martian went on to become a great producer of artists such as Donna Summers and Christopher Cross. I also starred in the musical, *Festival of Pentecost*, and played the role of Pastor Seymour, one of the founders of the Pentecostal Movement. I believe it was written by Rich Cook and the song, *He's Here Right Now* was in that musical and later became a popular song for Andrus, Blackwood, and Company.

I met Jon Stemkoski at a production of *Show Me* at a Baptist church in Bakersfield, California, where he was the producer at the age of 17! I had been hired to sing in the performance and he and I became great friends. He went to Visalia, California and formed a group called The Celebrant Singers, much like Thurlow Spur and The Spurlows. The Celebrant Singers traveled all over the world singing Christian songs and giving their testimony. Each member had to raise their own support to travel and they took their music to the Catholic church. Jon was a friend of Mother Theresa and made a tremendous impact with his music ministry. I really enjoyed singing with The Celebrant Singers as a guest artist. Being around such great young people was truly inspiring!

The Imperials

My invitation to join The Imperials was a historical event in the life and history of Southern Gospel Music. Although it was 1972, little thought or attention was given to the fact that the Southern Gospel Music industry was highly segregated. As a new member of The Imperials, I broke the color barrier and brought an entirely new dimension to the field of gospel music. At that time, all the other premier Southern Gospel singing groups were white. There were black Gospel singers in groups like The Mississippi Mass Choir, or singers like Mahalia Jackson but none of the Southern Gospel groups were integrated. I remember at my first meeting with The Imperials it was understood that if things didn't work out, it was "no harm, no foul." I would just go back to my previous job....I had quit my job so there wasn't anything to go back to but that was our beginning point. We started to rehearse, and Terry taught me all the songs I would be singing with the group. We started to rehearse at Belmont College in Nashville and groups would saunter in and out and listen to us. Some walked out shaking their heads, implying this would never work. However, we kept rehearsing and I had fun because it was such a different style of music. I was enjoying the variety. Our first concert was at Belmont College, we had a great audience, and it went over very well. Nonetheless when we went on the road, I had more difficulty because the stage attendants would always try to stop me from entering the stage entrance with The Imperials. We were dressed in the same uniform, but they could not wrap their heads around the fact that I was an Imperial. In some circles, there were audible gasps when we took the stage. We became even more successful because we could do a variety of styles and we were incredibly attractive to the college aged audiences because of the make-up of the group. The strange thing is that down south, blacks were not very aware of the integration of The Imperials. In the northern part of the country there was greater awareness, and many people celebrated my becoming a part of The Imperials.

The loneliest time of my life came when I became a part of The Imperials in January 1972.

Andrae had always been fun and easy to work with. With The Imperials there were always issues. My salary each week with The Imperials was $200.00 before deductions. This was much less than I had been making at Travelers Insurance. Much of my time was spent alone in my motel room, or on long walks on Music Row. All the gospel groups had their offices on Music Row, including The Imperials. The Speer Family had their offices there as well. Rita Bleile was their secretary. She noticed that I was walking with apparently no place to go and she and her roommate, Beverly Nelson, befriended me. They would bring me food from home because they noticed I was eating 25 cent hamburgers from Crystals. Beverly worked for a country music magazine and wrote an article on me that was published in her magazine. The two of them booked dates for me in some local churches. Rita was a very accomplished pianist and became my accompanist. It was great fun and it also augmented my finances, enabling me to send more money home to Winnie and Sherman Jr. I was determined to get back to my calling as a Christian Music Minister, so I accepted the terms of The Imperials. I do believe that the "steps of a righteous man are ordered by God" and my greatest concern was for my wife and son. My room at the motel was paid for by The Imperials but not my food. The "love offerings" from those small congregations helped a lot and so did the food that Rita and Beverly supplied!

Rita is now Mrs. Rita Berger, and she and her husband, Don, are great friends of mine. Unfortunately, we have not been able to locate Beverly, and believe that she has passed away. The friends I have made on this journey have been one of life's greatest blessings!

Around that same time an ardent fan of The Imperials, Avalee Johnston, assisted me with transportation. She and her friend, Diane, were big fans of The Imperials. Avalee was the shyest of the two but we managed to communicate. She allowed me to use her car to get around Nashville. She is now Mrs. Avalee Suinema and is still a dear friend. All the ladies I mentioned, Rita, Beverly, Avalee and Diane had compassion for me and saw how lonely I was without Winnie and Sherman, Jr. I thank God for them and do not believe I would have made it during that time without them. Nashville was a very segregated city in 1972 and they literally risked their reputation and livelihood by befriending me.

During the years I spent with The Imperials we were able to work with several well-known television personalities. One of those was Jimmie Dean. Two months each year we were in Las Vegas working with him at the Desert Inn. It was also during this time that Winnie and I became friends with Elvis Presley. Jimmy always found time to take Winnie, Sherman Jr., and me to dinner. He was incredibly kind to us. I used multiple opportunities to witness to him about Christ. He would always say, "you got to watch those Christian boys." Jimmy did 52 syndicated television shows. He decided to give each one of us 1% of the net profit from the shows. The owners of The Imperials, Joe Moscheo, Armond Morales, and Jim Murray went to him and tried to convince him to just give a lump sum and they would decide what they would give to Terry Blackwood and me. Of course, Jimmy declined because he wanted to be fair to all of us. I am sure they did not know that he told me about it. As I look back, I am so sad at how they limited their Christian influence because of their desire to make more money. Jimmy was extremely fair to all of us!

We also had the pleasure of working with Carol Channing of "Hello Dolly" fame. We backed her up at John Ascuaga's Nugget, a hotel in Reno, Nevada. We also were with her in Cleveland, Ohio at the Orange Blossom Festival. It was the most fun I ever had on stage because we had to dance on songs like, "Hello Dolly!" and "Diamonds Are A Girls' Best Friend." They hired a choreographer to work with The Imperials on our dance moves, supposedly in just a few days! Every night there was a tragedy, and we were just awful. We laughed so much at each other and we just could not dance! I can move on stage but if you choreograph me, I am dead meat. At the end of the show, we were supposed to be kneeling and one of us would be kicking! We could sing but we could not dance! An incredibly fun engagement with The Imperials!

One day Dorothy McGuire, a member of the McGuire sisters, and the girlfriend of Sam Giancana, invited all of us out to Sam's home for dinner. She had invited Florence Henderson and Tom Jones to attend as well. Larry Gatlin was substituting for Terry Blackwood in The Imperials at that time and we were all extremely impressed with Sam's mansion. He had six bungalows behind the main house, and they all had their own pool! It was the most elaborate place I have ever visited. The fact that Sam was a known mafia boss also made the dinner quite interesting. It was an eclectic group to say the least. Never a dull moment with Elvis.

Unfortunately Terry and I were not always treated fairly. For example, in Jimmy's contract there was a provision that if you cancel within 30 days of the event, you had to pay his total fee. He had a cancellation on one event, so he paid the group their fee. However, the group did not pay Terry nor me. Our agreement with the group was that we would get paid at every appearance. The fact that they got paid even though they did not sing did not bother them at all. Terry and I just had to live with their decision even though it was not a fair deal.

During the taping of one of Jimmy's shows I met Oprah Winfrey. She was around 18 years old and read the noon news at WLAC, Channel 5, Nashville, Tenn. We became friends and I sang at her uncle's church. One day I took her out to the car to meet Winnie. However, Winnie was having a "bad hair" day and didn't want to see anybody! Boy has she regretted that decision! I told Oprah I believed she had a great future for I had never met anyone so young, articulate, and poised.

Another highlight of my time with The Imperials was traveling with Pat Boone and his family. I loved touring Canada with him and his family because when The Imperials traveled by themselves, we always had trouble with Customs; we had to have a perfect count for everything, serial numbers for instruments, etc. It took hours! With Pat Boone we just went through with no problems. All they wanted was a picture with him! It was great! We opened the concert for him, and this provided a wonderful opportunity to get to know him in a personal way. The girls, Laurie, Debby, and Cherry were so much fun. Laurie's nickname for me was Hershey. I reconnected with Debbie in Atlanta at a book seller's convention several years ago and it was great to renew our friendship. I didn't think she would remember me, but she was so gracious, and I so appreciated that. I grew up listening to Pat Boone, Elvis Presley, Frank Sinatra, Fats Domino, Tony Bennet, Little Richard, and Sam Cooke to name a few! At our home we were allowed to listen to different kinds of music as long as the lyrics were clean. Music chronicled our lives. It's impossible to go through life and not hear the major performers. I loved Pat Boone's love songs, such as *Love Letters in the Sand* and *April Love.* I enjoyed the songs that others did but he stood out because he is the only artist I know that had success in the secular world and at a Christian concert could sing secular songs because his life was so exemplary. There were other secular artists who became Christians but unfortunately, they were driven away by audiences who were judgmental. Artists like Bob Dylan and B.J. Thomas were criticized if they tried to sing their secular songs at a religious concert. They were not allowed to be who they were but were always being pushed into a mold that stifled their creative genius. Pat Boone successfully navigated these channels of hypocrisy and was loved by all.

In 1974 Winnie and I vacationed in Hawaii. I had an opportunity to sing and do a television show for Wailai Baptist Church in Honolulu. I talked with Bill Smith, the pastor, and although the church was not large, he brought The Imperials to Hawaii for a week. I didn't ask for a booking fee; I was glad to get the group to Hawaii to minister.

I was blessed to do six albums with The Imperials and the first one was titled, The Imperials. The songs were written by Stevie Wonder, Carole King, and Kris Kristofferson. It would have been perfect in this day and age but at that time it was frowned upon because the writers were secular, and the lyrics rarely mentioned the Father, Son and Holy Ghost. The music and the vocal performances were excellent, but our audience was not ready for that. The album that really brought us into the mainstream and enhanced our popularity was The Imperials Live In Richmond, Indiana. The songs that became a staple of The Imperials were *More Than You'll Ever Know* by Jim Murray, *Light at The End Of The Darkness* by Terry Blackwood, and *Jesus Made Me Higher* by Sherman Andrus. It was our biggest seller.

The album that secured our Grammy was *No Shortage.* Gary Paxton wrote the song and produced the album. I was the lead singer on that song. I really didn't make any changes, but I simply copied the demo Gary had sent us to the "T". I learned with Andrae to sing the songs as closely to the way the writer wants them to be sung and have continued to do that throughout my career. The writer knows how the song should sound and the singer should honor that as much as possible. In my time with The Imperials, we had four Grammy nominations, but I only received three plaques. I believe the plaque for the last album, *Just Because*, was given to Russ Taff because I never received it.

It was an exciting time for all of us! We were traveling on a real bus instead of the Ford Econoline van! With The Imperials I had a bunk, a real driver, and hotel rooms when we were traveling, two to a room! When I first joined The Imperials, no one wanted to room with me. I had to room with the drummer, Gary McDuff. I didn't know what the guys thought of me and he would tell me what the guys would say when I wasn't around. They joked about not wanting to be around me with all the curly hairs in the sink! I was a loner, and it didn't bother me at all. For a short period of time, I roomed with Armond, I guess because he was a "mixed blood", Filipino and Irish, the lot fell to him. Armond really showed me the ropes. He had a routine he went through, and I learned the tricks of the road because of him. He was truly experienced because he had started traveling with The Weatherfords many years ago. Armond was the only one who had been in the military, so he was more comfortable being with people from different backgrounds and ethnicities. The Imperials were more organized and had more structure than we had in The Disciples however there were never long-term goals, just six months to a year. I believe that was a detriment because we had an incredible singing group that really impacted not only fans but other gospel groups. If we had implemented long term goals, we could possibly have had the same impact, popularity, and notoriety as The Oak Ridge Boys. We could hold our own with any group musically. One time I was in the elevator with The Statler Brothers, and they told me that in their opinion we were the best singing group in Nashville.

When I first joined The Imperials, Terry was a little skeptical about me because he was very conservative and had grown up in Mississippi. I would not have been able to travel with them without Terry's help. The Imperials had no charts so Terry would play harmonies for me and teach me the baritone part. I would record them and learn them by memory. Their arrangements were quite different than what I had learned in black gospel. In black gospel the baritone never went above the lead singer but that was not the case in Southern gospel. Terry received no extra pay for his work with me, but I learned so much from him and will be forever grateful. After being with me for a while, it became obvious that I was more conservative than Terry because of my upbringing in the Pentecostal church. For instance, we were not allowed to say to someone, "You are a liar!" That was like a profanity to my family. Instead, we would say, "You are telling a story." After a while we became close friends because we had similar upbringings.

The Imperials did a lot of touring in the Scandinavian countries like Sweden and Norway. It was interesting because some of the places where we went, the people had never seen a black person before, but they wanted to touch my skin. They were curious, not mean, or prejudicial. They loved our music, and many did not speak a lot of English yet responded greatly. We did autographs at the end of the concert; a first for me! The people were gracious and another one of my dreams came true as I traveled to places I had only dreamed about. We were not living in luxury and had austere accommodations, but we were greatly blessed to be there! We were brought into these countries by The Samuelson brothers who also had a singing group. They made a lot of money on us. Terry and I were just employees, but the group received a flat fee. I used to joke with them and tell them that if they could, they would have us do a concert in the baggage area to get their money's worth from us.

In those countries, their perception or beliefs were different from ours. Drinking wine with a meal was common and drinking "Christian" beer, (less alcohol) was also available. None of us participated in consuming any alcohol because of our beliefs. The important thing is we all believed in Christ and were committed to serving Him.

Another major event with The Imperials was the concerts we did at Del City First Baptist Church and The Starlight Crusades. This crusade lasted approximately a week and our wives and families were with us. These concerts were the highlight of our year. The two pastors that we worked with were Jimmy Draper and Bailey Smith. The music minister was Aubie McSwain. He is still a dear friend of mine. These were our best crowds of the year and we developed a lot of friendships with the people in Oklahoma. I never dreamed I would ever live in Oklahoma, but I love the people. They are the most supportive people I have ever been around.

The Imperials judged the success of their concerts by standing ovations. Jim Murray always had a song that engendered a standing ovation, for example, *Bridge Over Troubled Waters*. The second most popular song was *More Than You'll Ever Know*. If we had a concert and Jim did not get a standing ovation, in his opinion, we had a terrible concert. Joe Moscheo was the emcee and if we had a concert where the people were not responsive and enthusiastic, he would say during the team meeting, "Somebody dropped the ball." I'm the new kid in town and I'm feeling all this pressure that perhaps it was my fault. There was never any time to relax. Things were always tumultuous. When Joe had a good crowd, he talked a lot. When he had a bad crowd, he played a lot of music. Not a very pleasant time for anyone. In The Disciples, we gauged our success on the number of people who came to know the Lord. A vastly different standard, don't you think?

When I first joined the group Joe and Armond asked me for suggestions for improving the group. I told them I would suggest that we share personal testimonies. They said, they tried it before, and it doesn't work! I said, it's not supposed to work but rather a statement of why you do what you do! I then started giving my testimony and there was some resistance to that, but the crowd liked it! Before I joined, they did not give invitations to people to come forward to invite Christ into their life. I began giving invitations at the end of the concert, and people responded well. We ended all our concert with *I've Decided to Follow Jesus*. Armond stated in several interviews that my joining The Imperials was a spiritual turning point for the group. I have always known my limitations and I have always been free to compliment others. All the guys in The Imperials were great singers and I have no reservations about saying that. I never considered myself a great singer, but I always wanted to be a versatile singer. That was my reason for leaving Andrae and joining The Imperials. I simply challenged myself to be able to sing their style.

When Terry left the group in 1976, he said he was going home to help his mom because his dad had just passed away. His other reason was that he felt he could do all I did on stage, the ministry aspect of The Imperials, and he wanted to be able to do that as well. The fact is he was with The Imperials four years before I got there, and he never did the things I did. He is a gifted person, and I could never do some of the things he did, but I did not begrudge him. I simply did the things God called me to do. I think that one of the greatest weaknesses of the group was a competitive spirit and it stalled our progress. It was all about personal popularity not about ministry.

The Imperials, Dove And Grammy Award Winners: Terry Blackwood, Sherman Andrus Sr., Armond Morales, Jim Murray, Jeff Catron, Mike Kinnard, John Lutz, & Chuck Wright

Shalom Records

I left The Imperials in October of 1976, after spending five years and eight months with the group. I moved my family to Oklahoma City to run a record label, Shalom Records. The owner was Joe Stevens. I was excited about going there because of the caliber of talent in the Oklahoma City area. Hadley Hockensmith was a great guitarist and song writer. Harlan Rogers was a great pianist and songwriter. Bruce Hibbard, Kelly Willard, and Bobby Cotton were also great musicians, songwriters, producers, and engineers. I did two solo albums for Shalom Records using all those artists. The first album I did was *Soon Coming* and a lot of the songs were written by Harlen Rogers, Hadley Hockensmith, and Bruce Hibbard. Bobby Cotton was the producer. One of the songs we did on that album, *If You Abide in Me*, we put on the Andrus, Blackwood, and Company Live Album.

The song, *Father Me* was another of my favorites. I used to sing it on television for my son, Sherman Andrus Jr. with the Feed The Children Organization. I also traveled to Haiti with them and sang it there as well as at an orphanage. I felt like the ministry of Feed The Children was so great, I offered my talent since I was short on cash! I gave them the rights to the song I wrote, *Steal Away To Jesus*. I couldn't give them songs that others wrote but I could give them mine. The second album was, *How The Years Pass By*. I liked everything on that album but unfortunately the albums were not released, they escaped! . On that particular album I started relying on my ability to create vocal arrangements and that gave me confidence to do more writing. I worked there for about three months but needed to go back on the road to make a living because I was just a figure head and not able to make any decisions. God did bless me on the road however and I prospered under His leadership.

Andrus, Blackwood and Company

Soldiers Of The Light, 1980, Terry Blackwood & Sherman Andrus Sr.

Andrus, Blackwood and Company

In March 1977, the Benson Company called Terry Blackwood and asked him to talk to me about forming a group with the two of us. The Benson Company had lost The Imperials to Word Records out of Waco, Texas, a much larger record company. They wanted Terry and me to fill the void that had been left with the loss of The Imperials. They knew we were former members of The Imperials and that we could sell to the same demographic that had supported them. Neither one of us wanted to travel in a group again but we decided to give it a try. Our first album, *Grand Opening*, did very well. So, we formed a group and started booking concerts. An interesting tidbit, we got our name, Andrus, Blackwood, and Company through a contest put on by Benson! The winning submission was Andrus, Blackwood, and Company because the company was behind us.

We stayed together from 1977 through 1986. We were affectionately known as "ABC" and recorded five albums for the Benson label. Our biggest seller was *Soldiers of the Light,* however, the *ABC Live Album,* from Evansville, Indiana is the one that put us on the map! We had several hits on that album and the biggest one was *Jesus, You're So Wonderful*. It was a fun song, very comedic and people simply loved it. That album put us in a strong royalty bargaining position when Benson was thinking of selling their company. We were one of the top groups on the label and they wanted to make sure they kept us. They gave us a $60,000 bonus with $10,000 up front and then monthly installments for the remainder. To this day this is the most money I have ever made in one fell swoop in the music industry. God is good and His blessings are amazing!

Jesus, You're So Wonderful was written by Steve Fromm. His forte was 1950's songs and it was great fun to sing. We were at the Ichthus Festival and people knew us from The Imperials but did not recognize the name, Andrus, Blackwood, and Company. As we sat in the stands, the announcer began to call out the names of the performers for the following day and the people would scream and go crazy. When he said, "Andrus, Blackwood, and Company" no one said or did anything. This was disappointing but I turned to the group and said, "Don't worry they will know us when we leave here." I had no idea how prophetic that statement was! I love to have fun on the stage, and I would draw on my experiences of hearing R & B greats and seeing them perform. The next day we took the stage and had done a couple of up-tempo songs and I was thinking about James Brown and how he would dance around the stage and the stagehands would try to calm him down…creating an atmosphere of excitement. So, I started playing to the audience and told them that we had left Nashville hurriedly and were unable to bring our security folks with us.

I said that we were being cautious because we were such a popular group, people would rush the stage, trying to get to us and pull on our clothes and such….I was making up this story…Terry is standing behind me whispering, "Don't do that Sherm! Don't do that!" I kept going and I admonished them, "Please do not rush the stage!" That was like saying "Sic em!" to a dog. We started singing *Jesus, You're So Wonderful* and they all went crazy. I was prancing around. Terry was playing the straight man, muttering "Wonderful!" The people loved it and at the end, they rushed the stage! A great time was had by all and that was the song that put us on the map! The very next day, during our set, it started to rain. I made this bold proclamation, "I have the perfect song to sing. It's entitled, *Oh What A Lovely Day*. I told the assembled multitude that if we sang this song, the clouds would clear, and the rain would stop. We sang and the clouds cleared, the rains stopped, and the Christian papers wrote about the miracle. We not only acquired new fans, but our ministry took on a life of its own. It added immensely to our popularity.

ABC was made up of Terry Blackwood, my singing partner, and others. He is a great singer and he never got enough credit for his ability as a singer and an arranger. I have always admired his voice. At that time, we had Bob Villarreal on guitar and vocals, John Mays on bass and vocals, Karen Voegtlin on the keyboard and vocals and Billy Blackwood on the drums. Phil Johnson was our producer.

In 1980 we were the number one group in radio air play. In 1981 Terry married Cheryl Pruitt, a former Miss America. She made more money in gospel music than anybody we had ever seen. It was quite easy for her and Terry started touring with her, doing concerts and Amway gatherings. They had a television show on TBN called Together in Love. Unfortunately, there was never any mention of Terry and Andrus, Blackwood, and Company. Our popularity took a nosedive. Two years later they were divorced. Terry and I tried to revive our popularity but it was too late.

Prison Ministries

From 1986-2003 I did a lot of work as a soloist. I loved doing mission work and was privileged to travel to Poland, India, and all through the Caribbean Islands. In 1992 I received a call from Jesse Dixon, and he invited me to become a part of the Chuck Colson Prison Fellowship. I really enjoyed prison ministry! I sang in minimum- and maximum-security facilities. Some of the prisons I visited were Ryker's Island in New York, Angola in Louisiana, Huntsville in Texas, San Quentin, Tehachapi, and Folsom prison in California. I was with Chuck Colson on several Easter services in different prisons. I so enjoyed working with him because he was a man of great integrity. He had a photographic memory and was brilliant. Before he and I connected he had done time in prison. He had worked with President Richard Nixon and was caught up in the Watergate scandal and went to prison for his role.

While he was there, he noticed that all the ministries that came in assumed that all the prisoners needed someone to preach to them. He realized that they also needed clean entertainment! When he was released, he founded Prison Fellowship and featured singers, comedians, body builders, ex-football players and other people who simply wanted to share their love of Christ with the prisoners. He raised money through corporations and enabled us to put-on first-class ministries for the inmates. It remains a successful program and is still going strong even though Chuck Colson has gone to be with his Lord. I really enjoyed being a part of that ministry and believe I helped make a difference! My simple message was that God protected me from a life of sin because I gave my heart to him at an early age.

One song that they requested more than any other was *One More Night With The Frogs*. I wrote that song while listening to Dr. E.V. Hill preach from Exodus, chapter eight, when Pharaohs summoned Moses to remove the plague of the frogs. Moses asked Pharaoh when he wanted God to remove the frogs and Pharaoh replied, "Tomorrow." I listened to Bob Marley quite a bit to capture the Reggae sound. Apparently, it worked! It was a hit at every location.

As a matter of fact, I was brought in for a special banquet at Broad River Correctional facility to especially sing, *One More Night With The Frogs(1987)*. I have been blessed to minister at all levels of the prison system. We had a lot of people who were extremely popular in contemporary Christian music at that time ministering along with us such as Kathy Traccoli and Steven Curtis Chapman. I especially remember working with Steven Curtis Chapman at one facility. Prior to the service he and I spent about forty-five minutes singing Andrus, Blackwood, and Company songs. He was a big fan of ABC and remembered seeing Terry and me as a young man in his hometown of Paducah, Kentucky. He was scheduled to close the program that night, but he told the person in charge that he wanted me to close it out. I will always remember his kindness and genuine love of our music.

One of the most enjoyable times I had ministering was when I worked with Demond Wilson of Sanford and Son in 1989. He was the speaker for an outdoor meeting in Trinidad-Tobago. I did the music, and he shared his testimony. He had only known Christ as Savior for a short time and as they say, he was on fire for God! He had a no-nonsense approach to the Gospel. Once the services were over, we would retire to his suite. He would loosen up and begin to tell us funny stories. He could do a lot of different voices and dialects. He and Jimmy Dean were alike in that they each had that unique ability. There was always a lot of food present too, so we enjoyed our time together.

The Lord continued to open doors for me to minister in prisons and I was blessed to work with Mr. Andy Eden. His ministry was in California and we met through mutual friends, The Gospel Messengers. They were all living in New York. Michael and Nathan Duncanson and their families did so much to support my ministry! I will always be indebted to them.

Ministry on the Road-Solo

After leaving The Imperials I did many different solo gigs. I had multiple opportunities through a variety of sources. I did a lot of churches and youth groups. I did one of the first cruises sponsored by The Church of The Nazarene for lay people. Jim Russom was one of the coordinators and happened to be our neighbor in Oklahoma City. Our sons, Sherman Jr., and Mark were classmates in Putnam City West High School. I also did cruises with Jesse Dixon and several Elvis Cruises. Those cruises were filled with Elvis fans and we were paid handsomely!

I continued to do solo albums, one with Amethyst Recording Studio; *Caution To The Wind* and one with Exodus Records, *Seize The Moment. Caution To The Wind* was one of my most successful albums with *One More Night With The Frogs* becoming the most requested song of my career. The kids call me "The Frog Man"....just a little embarrassing!

It was a blessing to participate in ministry trips to other countries which included a trip to Africa with my pastor, Ron Dryden. The Lord opened doors for me to minister in Poland, Germany, and England as a soloist. It was a little more difficult as a soloist, but I really got to know the people because I often stayed with them in their homes.

On my trip to Poland, I went from Frankfurt to Warsaw. In the airport only two languages were spoken, German and Polish. When I landed in the airport in Warsaw, the airport was named WARSZAWA. It was pronounced very differently. I knew I was at the right place because everyone got off the plane...including me. At Customs they were simply concerned about how much money I was bringing in because I could not take out more money than I brought in. Poland was the most dangerous country I visited. I was there for three weeks and I did not know anyone there, nor did I speak the language. When I arrived, I went to stay in the home of the young man who was my drummer. The only one who spoke even a little bit of English was his wife. It made for interesting conversations. I realized that anything could happen to me and no one would know because no one knew where I was or who I was. While in Poland I developed a whole new understanding of Catholicism. My very first concert in Poland I met a priest and he told me that what Poland needed was holiness, from top to bottom. One of the issues facing the church was the desire of priests to marry. I heard several discussions on that topic. Their churches were filled with people who appeared to be seriously seeking Christ and it was a blessing to minister to them through music. In the concerts in Poland, all of the money was given to the band. I was there simply to minister! Our advertisements for the concert were pictures of me on posts throughout the countryside. Everyone wanted to see a black man from America and hear the music but even more importantly, they wanted to hear my testimony, my walk with God! It wasn't all about show biz but rather about the things of the Lord. What a blessing and how refreshing! Politically, everyone would want to take me to Warsaw and point at a building that was built by the Russians with money from the Polish people. It was supposed to be a token of friendship between the Polish and Russians, but the Polish people were upset because it had been built with their money.

On another note, when I wanted to talk with Winnie, I had to go to a building with phones, insert a pre-paid phone card and talk until the money ran out. How times have changed!

The Lord opened the door for me to sing at the Nazarene World Congress for thousands of young people. One night I noticed a young lady who looked absolutely devastated. I went to her after the concert and began to talk with her. She told me that her dad died, and she did not want to be there. I said, "Well, why don't you let me be your dad this week." She said, "Ok!' Robin Elliott Barnett became my daughter that week and we have had a lifetime of friendship. She does not miss getting in touch with Winnie and me on every holiday and many times simply calls out of the blue. She always reminds me of the difference I made in her life. She regrets not getting to meet Sherman Jr. because she always wanted to tell him "Thanks!" for sharing his parents with her. She is happily married with a family of her own and is truly a daughter to us.

I also had the opportunity to go to Guyana with Pastor Tony Fontanelle. Earlier I had sung in his church in New York City and we'd had a great time. Every year he planned a return trip to Guyana to encourage the churches and pastors. He invited me to go with him and this was the area where the Jonestown/Jim Jones incident had taken place years earlier. The atmosphere was totally oppressive and dark, but Pastor Fontanelle wanted to shine a light to encourage the believers! I, along with Madeline Mims Jackson, went and we had a wonderful time under the anointing of the Holy Spirit. The ladies had a great place to stay but we, the men, had to stay in a place where we had netting to keep out the mosquitoes and take cold showers! Pastor Fontanelle was shocked that I did not ask to go to a hotel! There were such wonderful people in Guyana!

In 1972, while working with The Imperials, I met Peggy Stark who has since become Dr. Peggy Stark-Wilson. At that time, she lived in Oklahoma but came to our concert in Indiana with a friend she was visiting. She approached me after the concert, and we began to talk about ministering in small churches. She asked me if I ever considered singing in small churches and ministering to young people in a more personal way. I remember being very flippant with her, and said, "What's in it for me?" She said, "You'll get your reward in heaven." We both laughed and that was the beginning of a lifelong friendship. She invited me to Boynton, Oklahoma to sing for the community where she taught school. I was finally able to go and sing for them and met some wonderful students who have since gone on to successful careers and ministry. One of the young ladies I met was Marva Walker. She had a great voice and later sang on my album, *Seize The Moment*. She is actively involved in ministry at World Won For Christ in Tulsa, OK.

Peggy moved to Texas in 1973 to teach school in San Antonio and was excited to be able to schedule concerts for me in Texas, in small churches. It was exactly what I wanted to do but didn't know how to get started. We started at The Eastside Church of the Nazarene where I met Pastor Leonard Adams, known as "The Preacher." He was a great supporter of mine until he passed away.

Peggy and Pat Eskew, her friend, and I had many comical experiences because I wasn't doing concerts to raise money for myself but rather to help the church, especially the young people. I remember one church in particular where I sang for a young people's service. At the most we had 30 people that evening. The pastor picked up a love offering and took it to his office. After the service, he invited me to the office. He laid the offering out on his desk and he said, " We have $13.50, how do you want to split it brother?" I thought it was the funniest thing I had ever heard. I just smiled and said, "That's ok. You keep it pastor." And he did! That's when you know you haven't done a good job! Not even worth $13.50!

One of my great blessings from my friendship with Peggy was getting her family as my own. Her parents and her whole family treated us as if we were a part of their family. Winnie, Sherman Jr., and I realized that Peggy's mom and dad did not see color but just people. Marilyn Stark, her sister, serves as Oklahoma State Legislator for District 100 and is like that as well. We have shared many dinners together and many great conversations. The Starks are genuine and caring, not seeing anything but love. I have so appreciated their support over the years and consider them my extended family.

An additional aspect of my ministry was chaplaincy at Southern Nazarene University. A man named Doug Schlabach came to one of our concerts and talked to Coach Gresham and asked him if it would be ok to have me become the chaplain for the athletic department. He said yes and I then had the privilege of working with the men and women's basketball teams. The men were highly supported by their fans and were at the top of their game. The women were up and coming and I would go to all the games and sing the National Anthem. I have great memories of all the different players who played during that time.

Winnie and I became Mom and Dad. I would go out for the weekend and come home on Sunday night and there would be long, tall people sleeping all over my floor. Winnie loved to cook for everybody but didn't get started till after midnight! All the players were brothers and sisters to Sherman Jr. Those were some of the best years of our lives. The boys were always competitive, but the girls went on to win the National Championship in 1989. One of my all-time favorites is Katrina Springer. She is my biggest fan, and I am her smallest supporter. She too is family to us. She is such a mild-mannered person until she got on the basketball court then she became a terror at a mere 6'5!

I have kept up with several of the basketball players; KP Westmoreland, Vernon Coleman, commonly known at Little V, Vernon Johnson, commonly known as Big V and James Carson. I still talk with them quite often and they always thank us for all we did for them. They believe they would not have made it without our acceptance, love, and support. I never lost my love for sports and even worked with the OKC Thunder for two years so that I could see every team in the NBA at least once. I worked as an usher and it was the hardest job I have ever had!

In 1988, I began my ministry in Alaska with a visit led by the State Overseer for The Church of God, Rev. Grissom. The Grissom family was my host, but I also met Allen and Miriam Humphries and there was an instant chemistry. They had a church in Soldotna and invited me to minister. Our friendship grew and over the years I have had the privilege of producing three albums for Miriam. Over a period of several years, I went two to three times a year to Alaska and ministered in churches and at conferences. Every Christmas I did a concert in Soldotna. I became such a part of the community that I was a special guest for Soldotna High School Prom. I was the only adult besides the sponsors! For some reason I hit it off with the kids and it was like I was living my teenage years all over again. Whenever I returned for a concert, the kids would all come to church for the concert even when they weren't regular church goers. I sometimes led worship with Miriam and even did the youth services downstairs. My crowds were bigger than the worship service. I was 50 at the time and I was having a "second childhood!" Mark and James, the Humphries sons, always involved me in their activities and kept me young. They are like a second family to me.

While I was there, I met a young woman who was an Aleut Indian. Her name was Dawana and she was very shy and was threatening to quit school. I told her that if she finished high school, I would be on the front row for graduation. I became good friends with her family and attended her graduation. She is married now and lives in California. At her graduation, another young lady came up and asked me to mentor her like I had Dawana. I told her I would have to speak with her family. Her parents were pastors of a church in Kenai and they were happy to have me befriend her and mentor her. Her name is Amy, and we are still friends. I lost track of her for 23 years, but we reconnected a few years ago. She convinced her children that I was a long-lost grandfather. She has been widowed twice but has continued to trust the Lord and her love for music has never wavered. My schedule was full on one of my trips to Alaska and I really didn't have the time or opportunity to connect with her. However, she called Winnie and found out where I was visiting and tracked me down. She has remained a close part of our family.

On one occasion she and her family were traveling through Memphis and the children wanted to go to Graceland. She told them, "I bet your grandfather, Sherman, could make that happen." She called me and I made some calls, and they were able to visit Graceland, with complimentary tickets. I did not realize that I still had any influence with the Elvis representatives at Graceland, but they all remembered me and let me know that I was quite the celebrity there. You may find it strange that I always have young ladies seeking me out as a father figure. Winnie says it is because I always wanted a daughter. I think it is because I look pitiful and the ladies want to help me. I even have great ladies who have taken me on as their project at work, supplying me with food and encouragement every week.

Over the years I have been invited to participate in the Gaither Video series. Our first one was in Indiana and I did a couple of lines from songs. I was just getting acquainted with everyone. In New Orleans I did *Precious Lord* and have received many compliments on that rendition. The song was not in my key and when there was a key change it was too high. I decided that I was going to do it anyway because I did not want to refuse. I thought if I said it was too high, I would never be invited back by Bill Gaither. I was determined to sing it and the tenor, Gordon Stoker of the Jordanaires, told me I had done a great job. However, my favorite was at Carnegie Hall when we sang *A Few Good Men*. It was extremely well done and so patriotic. I loved being there and doing my part to honor our first responders at 911. I sat in the audience with Lanelle Harris and he said, "What do you think about these things?" I said, "I'd rather be in a small church!" He said, "So would I!" I have never felt comfortable being around lots of other artists because it feels like everyone is jockeying for position. Sandi Patty is one of my favorite singers and I loved the duets that she and Larnelle did! They always held their audiences spell bound! I was glad that they set such a high standard for their duet performances. There were several songs that I was the first to record and Larnelle recorded them as well: *Questions* and *Father Me*. The primary difference was that they were a major third higher for him and we chuckle about that!

I really did not know Sandi Patty well at that time, but Karen Voegtlin, a member of Andrus Blackwood, and Company mentioned her to me one day when we were talking about unique voices. Sandi appealed to such a wide audience because of the magnificence of her voice. Her voice became her moniker. It was an understatement because of her incredible range. She also signed as she sang and that was totally different. What really put her over the top in the music industry was when she did the Star-Spangled Banner on ABC for the Statue of Liberty

Rededication on July 6, 1986. She became a household name! Peter Jennings, the anchor, wanted to know who she was, and that performance opened a whole new area for her. Whitney Houston had done an amazing job on The Star-Spangled Banner at the Super Bowl, but it was prerecorded. Sandi Patty sang it live and she was magnificent! I was immensely proud, as a Gospel music artist, to have someone of her caliber represent the Gospel Music industry in the secular world.

Jake Hess was a wonderful man and made me feel more than welcome! He was a fan of mine from the time I joined The Imperials, and he was the first Southern Gospel singer to invite me into his home when I moved to Nashville. I met Kelly Willard at that time because she was playing the piano for the Jake Hess Trio. Ray Walker of the Jordanaires also made me feel welcome in Nashville by inviting me to his home for dinner and just to hang out.

I have made a lot of mistakes in my time. I have made statements I have come to regret. For example, "the Beatles were just a flash in the pan." There were other things that I tried that just did not work for me. A good friend of mine, Leon Patillo, came to my home in Oklahoma City. I didn't know he was checking me out because he had met a lot of flakes in gospel music. He loved my family and whenever he came to town, he invited us to the concert and would visit in our home whenever he could. Several years later he told me about a hairdresser named Jannelle. She had his hair looking great. He encouraged me to go see her because I was starting to lose my hair. That was one of the biggest mistakes of my life. I had a hair weave, and it caused my hair to fall out even more!

One of my biggest regrets came when I was living in Hawaii. One of my best friends, Carol Majeau, became ill and I had known her and her husband since she was 17. I knew her entire family but when I was told she was terminal; I just froze and did not respond and did nothing. That still haunts me to this day!

Imperials Part II

In 1997 Graceland started doing a show called Elvis: The Concert. It was Elvis on the big screen and all of us who had an affiliation with him were part of the live musicians and singers. I was chosen to participate because I had been a part of The Imperials. We did shows all over western Europe, Japan, and Australia. In Memphis, Terry Mike Jeffries, a great singer, would come in and do an Elvis tribute for a birthday celebration or for Elvis Week. He was a lot of fun to work with and he always invited me up to sing a solo during the concert. We were both fans of Wilson Pickett, a well-known blues singer and he would scream a lot! Yowww! Terry Mike and I would then have fun and scream at each other, "Help me!" which kept us both laughing through the concert….off mike of course! Ronny McDowell, a country singer, also loved to do Elvis songs and he was great fan of Sam Cook. We did several shows with him and on a special trip in Toronto, we backed him up. One evening he invited me up on stage and asked me to do Sam Cook's *You Send Me*….I brought the house down!

I also participated in two videos that are being sold on Public Television. The first video was, *He Touched Me*, and I was privileged to be a part of the 25th Anniversary Show. It was a great honor to be a part of the videos and the *Elvis, The Concert Tour*. My only regret was that I was not with The Imperials when they backed Elvis in Las Vegas.

As a result of our involvement in the Elvis tour, in 2003 we were invited to sing in Paris, France with Frank Michaels, a singer from Belgium. He had a show and Celine Dion's older sister, Claudia, was on stage with us. She did not speak much English, but her manager did. We had gotten the gig because we had provided back-up for Frank on his album, Thank You Elvis. He flew us and our wives to Paris for a month! Our concert hall was the Olympia, France's Carnegie Hall.

In 2004 a gentleman from Oklahoma named John purchased cemetery and mortuaries in Hawaii. He was a great fan of The Imperials. He remembered us from our concerts at The

First Southern Baptist Church in Del City, OK. We performed at the Starlight Crusade for many years. After purchasing these properties, he contacted our tenor, Jim Murray, to see if we would be interested in moving to Hawaii to represent his company in the Christian community. Of course, our answer was a resounding "Yes!" He offered us a sufficient salary and he moved our families, lock, stock, and barrel to Honolulu. We were so excited, especially our wives! Everything went smoothly the first few months, then we found out that he had misappropriated funds from a trust that was under investigation. He decided that our job was no longer to represent him in the community but to come in every day and pray for approximately eight hours a day that the investigation would end.

Jim and Armond were "Gung ho!" to do whatever John said. I always gave the dissenting opinion because I never believed you could correct wrong by praying it away. You need to "fess up" and repent! The prayers were so wild and ridiculous that one member, I won't name him, prayed that the Lord would somehow kill one of the commissioners who called for the investigation. I have never been involved in anything as crazy as this! Armond and Jim stood by John but distanced themselves from Terry and me. They actually thought that John would help them financially. Terry moved his family back to Nashville. Jim and Armond convinced Dave Will to move to Hawaii to take Terry's place. Despite all their efforts, the company dissolved, and everyone had to move back to Nashville. I stayed in Hawaii for four more years because, my beautiful wife, Winnie, loved it so much. During all the turmoil in Hawaii we put our trust in God. Through all of this I kept my composure and walked in faith with God. I view each member of The Imperials as associates but not as friends.

One of the blessings that came from our time in Hawaii was a song I wrote, *Living In Paradise Costs A Lot*. The Imperials went to California and did a week tour. During that time, we each made $5.000.00. I approached the group with a suggestion that we set up a group of tours. I said that we could be like The Cathedrals; fly in a couple of days early, rehearse, rent a bus, and then do a tour of dates. We wouldn't need a band because we could use tracks. If we planned to do a tour once a quarter, we could stay busy with the group and have our individual ministries the rest of the year. Armond and Jim looked at each other and said, "I don't want to ride a bus." I said you probably don't want to ride in a van either. I jokingly said that for the kind of money we could make, I would ride a skateboard! In my heart of hearts, I honestly believe they did not want to work with me. I am not sure what rubbed them the wrong way, but they never seemed to want to treat me as their equal. Jim and Armond went so far as to try to secure a patent on the name, The Imperials, but found out that it was already owned by Little Anthony and The Imperials. Terry confronted them and it was obvious that they did not want to include us in their endeavors. As life happens, I was in Alaska several months later doing concerts and The Imperials were in Alaska riding in a car and singing in the same size churches where I was performing as a soloist!

My second run with The Imperials ended in 2010. Joe Moscheo and Terry Blackwood decided that I did not need to make the same pay as they did on the Elvis show because I had not actually sung as backup with Elvis but was simply his friend. They decided they would take 10% off the top and then split the rest with me. They told me that all I did was sing, they did all the bookings. I told them that if all I do is sing, then all Kobe Bryant does is play basketball! The reason I compared myself to Kobe Bryant was because of my work ethic. There wasn't anyone who worked harder on stage than I did and that was the thing people always responded to—my energy level was contagious. The conductor of the Elvis show, Joe Guercio, told them they were lucky to have me along because I could always get the crowd going. In every situation, no matter the configuration of the group, it was always about finances. However, God always has a plan for His child, and He had a plan for me! Little did I dream that in 1998 I would be inducted into the Gospel Music Hall of Fame as a member of The Imperials and as a founding member of Andraé Crouch and The Disciples. God truly does reward those who diligently seek Him!

Andrus and Bingle

In 2002 I was ministering on the Vashon Island near Washington state and a young lady in the audience, Cindy Korenek, told me that I should get in touch with her pastor, Lonny Bingle. He pastored in Spokane Washington and she thought he would be interested in having me come to his church. I contacted him and I began doing concerts at Spokane Faith Center. Prior to this time, he had done a violin instrumental album produced by Terry Blackwood, *My Little World*. He and Terry were good friends and as I continued to minister at his church our friendship grew also. Lonny had been ministering in India for many years through his church and they supported churches there as well. He invited me to go on a tour of India with him and on the flight to India, he suggested that we write some songs together. I didn't want to do anything except sleep, but I acquiesced, and we started talking about some songs that I had on my mind. The first song I mentioned was *Think Upon These Things*. We started working together and we finished seven songs. I wrote the music and we both wrote the lyrics

In India we had a great time ministering in Amritsar, near the Pakistan border. We had a warm reception there and it was like being in another world altogether. It was very primitive, and it is against the law to baptize people, but we worshipped and prayed together. We had an outdoor concert scheduled but had to cancel it because the police found swords underneath the stage. Lonny was in charge but sent us all home. This was during the time when several missionaries were murdered and burned to death. It was somewhat dangerous, but the Lord continued to give us opportunities and people were hungry for the gospel. I am not a minister of the spoken Word, but I did preach several times while we were there. This ministry was more like my time with Andrae and The Disciples because the music was a vehicle, but the Word of God was the message. We felt an anointing of the Holy Spirit and people were healed and came to know Christ. Unfortunately, I was not feeling well the whole time I was there, but I didn't miss a single service or event.

When we got back to Spokane we talked with Lonny's brother, Karl Bingle. He had a recording studio and a label and we were interested in doing an album with him. We wrote the songs, went into the studio, and recorded them. We completed seven songs and then while in New York, I wrote two more songs. On the way home from a Prison Fellowship event, I wrote the final song. Between the two of us we had ten songs to record and *Think Upon These Things* became our first album together. We had reasonably good success with the album and began to book dates in Washington, Alaska, and Canada. The people liked our songs, all original, and we were operating without promotion. The churches where we performed were all places where I had been as a soloist and they welcomed us back.

The second album was a result of continued collaboration entitles, *A Servant's Heart*. It was all original material. We sent it to the Grammy committee, and it was on the ballot for 2014. I had not had anything on the Grammy's for 30 years and we were thrilled to attend the Grammy Award Show in Los Angeles at the Staple Center. We were in the nosebleed section, but we had fun. Lonny put on our website that we were going to The Grammys with a song on the ballot, and a former member of The Imperials responded with, "Is this the real Grammy's?"

In 2018 we did a live album in Oklahoma, *For Such A Time As This*. It has done well, and we paid to have it promoted. Unfortunately, COVID-19 hit and we have not been able to schedule any concerts. This album was the best produced live album that I have had the privilege to be a part of. My nephew, Lloyd Duplechan, was the producer and arranger. It is the best quality and has all original music. The concert was well attended, and we received enough in the love offering to pay all the musicians and vocalists. The album cost between $8,000.00 and $10,000. We were about $1800.00 short but my nephew, Lloyd and his wife, Jill, paid the balance so it is fully paid for! Lonny has been an inspiration to me and because he is very progressive, he has helped me on the creative side of my music. He is not satisfied with the status quo and he and his wife and family have been a tremendous support to me and to my wife, Winnie.

Sherman Andrus Sr. & Lonny Bingle

Elvis Presley

First, I want to say I never had the privilege to tour with Elvis Presley. I joined The Imperials after they were no longer working with Elvis. When I joined, they were working with Jimmy Dean. One evening Elvis asked the guys in The Imperials to bring me to his suite in Las Vegas. He wanted to meet me because I was the first guy to sing, *I've Got Confidence.* At the time I did not know it, but he wanted to make me a member of the "Memphis Mafia", his group of friends. He was very gracious and as in the case with Jimmy Dean, if he had objected to The Imperials hiring me, they would not have. The Imperials always thought they would get back with Elvis, but The Stamps really had it sewed up.

When I met Elvis, he gave me an embrace and a handshake and said, "Now, you are one of us." Immediately I started joking around with him and said, "Well, I hear all of your friends have a "TCB" necklace and I don't have one." I was just joking with him. He said, "I'm going to get you one!" A few days later at the Desert Inn as we were backing up Jimmy Dean, he came to the show just before the curtains opened and placed jewelry boxes in our hands. We were looking for a place to put them quickly and he thought that was extremely funny. We did the first set with Jimmy Dean, about fifteen minutes of music, and then retired to the Green Room. He was upstairs with his entourage laughing at us. When we opened the jewelry boxes, all the guys had a bracelet. In my jewelry box was a bracelet and a "TCB" chain. He kept his promise.

He was so respectful to women and children that I was able to take Winnie and Sherman Jr. up to his suite. We all sat around the piano and no one heard any profanity. I have a picture of us with him along with Mama Cass and it is a great memento. I loved being around him because the only other person who loved music as much as he did was Andrae Crouch.

Elvis sang more music off stage than on and he embraced all different styles. A lot of the songs he sang, like *C.C. Rider,* was done by Chuck Willis, a black artist, and I admired the way he took songs and made them his very own. His conductor, Joe Guercio, did not realize that the song, *I Got A Woman Way 'Cross Town* started out as a Gospel song, *It Must Be Jesus* by The Southern Tones. Ray Charles changed it to *I Got A Woman Way 'Cross Town* and recorded it as a rhythm and blues song. Elvis later recorded it and made it a rock and roll hit. Glen Hardin, pianist, and arranger for Elvis, did a wonderful job and it was a real joy to work with the TCB Band. Jerry Scheff, Ronnie Tutt, James Burton were great artists to work with. They are all legendary performers and should be in the Rock and Roll Hall of Fame. James Burton is! I also enjoyed getting to know and work with The Sweet Inspirations; Estelle Brown, Myrna Smith, Sylvia Shemwell and Portia Griffen. The only original member who is still living is Estelle Brown. I often sang on their songs when I wasn't singing with The Imperials and they were fun to travel with. They too should be in the Rock and Roll Hall of Fame. I enjoyed so much working with Joe Guercio and the group. Joe always talked about writing a book. I wish he had! He had the most storied history of all of us. Sadly, he is no longer with us. I especially loved to compete with him trying to "Name That Tune!" I even won a couple of times. As I look back, I am so impressed with the way Elvis treated all of them. I genuinely loved that about him!

When we were with Elvis in the suite, he did not want to sing Rock and Roll, he wanted to sing Gospel music. One day when we were singing an old hymn, Mama Cass who was there, began to cry. She told us that she had started her singing career in church with that song. She sang with us and she had a great voice. Elvis also liked romantic ballads. One evening he wanted to do the song, *Softly As I Leave You* made popular by Charles Boyer. It was both sung and recited. Unfortunately, we were the only two in the room who knew the song. I couldn't play the piano, and neither could he, however we tried our best with many starts and stops along the way. We both loved the song because the words were so beautiful.

Elvis was fun to be around because he was a practical joker. He was always practicing Karate on his valet. One of the funniest times was when Joe Moscheo's house in Nashville had been robbed. Elvis got on the phone and asked all his Karate friends to be ready to meet him in Nashville at Joe's house. He asked his valet to get his robe and he put it on. Dressed in his robe, along with his official J Edgar Hoover's badge and his gun, he took us all in his limo to Bali Hai motel to Joe's room to set up a command post. He didn't have his driver, so he grabbed the doorman and made him drive the limo. We are all in the limo and he clears his throat and spits on the floor. The driver turns around and looks at him and Elvis says, "What are you looking at? I can buy you and this car." No one went to Joe's house, but it was great fun, and I was laughing the whole time.

On a serious note, one evening he was showing me his latest album, *Live From Hawaii*. He was so excited to see all over the album cover, "We love Elvis!" in multiple languages. I told him that it was a God thing. I have never seen any artist as dearly loved as he and I believed it was ordained by God. He agreed with me. He was a very spiritual man. At one time he had us sit in a circle, hold hands in the dark, and repeatedly listen to my testimony and the song, *Jesus Made Me Higher*. He was intense and wanted everyone to focus on the message of the song.

On several occasions I sent him an invitation to attend Bible Studies on the strip in Las Vegas. Jim Reed was the chaplain of the Strip and he held Bible Studies on Tuesdays and Thursdays in between shows. The chorus girls would come in their costumes and were very frank in the questions they asked. They were incredibly open to hearing the Word because they did not know how to "fake it" since few had ever been in a church. Unfortunately, I don't think that the people closest to Elvis ever got the invitations to him. It would have been an honor to travel and work with him because I admired his love for music and his generosity. I genuinely believe that he was blessed with a special talent. I've never seen anyone live so long in the hearts and lives of people as Elvis Presley.

Terry Blackwood, Sherman Andrus, Sr., Jim Murray, Armond Morales,
Mama Cass, Marty Allen, Elvis Presley, Linda Thompson, & Joe Moscheo

Cancer Survivor!

In 2010 I received a diagnosis from the doctor that I had suspicious cells in my prostate. Because my older brother and father both had prostate cancer, the medical team recommended a pre-emptive strike; treat the cells as a precautionary measure. I had a biopsy done and it was the most painful procedure I have ever experienced. I began radiation treatments in May at Integris Medical Center. My doctor recommended 44 treatments. Thankfully, I had no serious side effects. I kept doing all the things I usually did but did have some night sweats.

During that time, I had someone on Facebook ask me if I remembered Dolores Ricard? I replied, "Of course, she was a girlfriend of mine while I was in college." The person replied, "That's me. I am Dolores Ricard" She told me that she had purposed in her heart to find me before she passed away and I thought that was an odd thing to say. We started communicating and she told me that as she read my bio, she realized that I had accomplished all I had said that I wanted to accomplish, and she was enormously proud of me for doing that. I had told her of my dreams and aspirations because I thought she was the girl I was going to marry. We were both eighteen years of age and too young to get married at that point. I went to California to live with my brother, Jim, and that's when my ministry really took off. Reconnecting was like I had found a long lost relative. She would check on me after my radiation treatments to encourage me. Winnie was aware that we were talking and knew that her encouragement was helpful. We discussed our families and at the end of my radiation treatment, she had to go in for surgery for her gall bladder. She found out it was cancerous. I regret that I was not able to do more for her. I could sense she was getting weaker and weaker when we talked on the phone. Winnie and I wanted her to come to Oklahoma because of our great medical facilities so she could get treatment, but it never happened. One Friday morning I got a call from one of her daughters and she told me that Dolores had passed away. I found out that Dolores' husband had died several years earlier, and her children had asked her if their dad was the person, she always thought she would marry, She told them "No, I thought I would marry Sherman Andrus." I drove to Louisiana for the funeral and I sat way in the back. I didn't want to cause any confusion and when the service was over, during the repast, her daughters came up to me and we talked together. That was one of the saddest things I have experienced.

At the time I was working as a valet. You are probably asking yourself, "Why would a Gospel singer be working for a valet company?" That's where it gets interesting! While driving Winnie for Integris for a check-up at Baptist hospital, I heard a commercial for Jenny Craig, stating that you only had to pay her one dollar for each pound that you lost." I looked at Winnie and said, "That's the dumbest thing I ever heard!" Winnie looked at me and said, "What do you mean?" I said, "Why should anyone pay Jenny Craig a dollar a pound to lose weight when they're the ones who need to lose the weight." "So", she said, "What would you do since you're so smart?" At that time, I saw some valets running around getting cars, I then said, "I would get a job that makes me lose weight! See those guys over there, those valets? I would do that!" She said, "You can't do that!" I said, "Watch me!" Linda Van Horn, one of the executives at Integris, saw me serving as a valet and invited me to come to Integris to work as a driver. I started working for them in November 2010 and celebrated a 10-year anniversary in November 2020. I enjoy driving people to and from their treatments because I can put them at ease. The diagnosis of cancer is very scary but when they realize that I have survived, they take comfort. I treat them all with kindness. They often wonder who I am because I don't dress like a normal driver. They inquire of the staff inside and when they find out who I am, many of them ask me to sing for them. They are shocked that someone who has allegedly accomplished as much as I, works with a servant's heart. I am not there to push any agenda but to simply be used of God to minister to them. Many of them have become my friends and often when they pass away, they want me to sing at their funerals.

Although there is a high rate of recovery still many don't make it. This impacts all of us at Integris because we are like one big family. I may come in after a weekend and learn that one of our clients has passed away. It makes us sad, but we are thankful we were able to help in some way. This is a ministry opportunity I never imagined. With my cancer God opened the door for me to minister to one of the most fragile and hurting parts of our community. Working at Integris has been a real joy because they all have the desire to serve. It is the best working environment I have experienced due to the support of all my co-workers. They worry about me getting enough to eat and getting enough rest. This has been especially true because they know about Winnie and her situation. God has used them to minister to me particularly in this time of COVID 19 quarantine.

Life with the Right Partner, Winnie Holman Andrus

Winnie is exactly who and what I needed as a life partner. She is extraordinarily strong willed and not a shrinking violet. She loved to travel and was extremely outgoing! When she met me, I was still somewhat shy. She taught me how to be friendly because she thought if I were unfriendly people would think I was trying to be uppity. At the concerts with Andrae, I would slide out the side door when we finished singing because I did not like to meet people. Winnie taught me how to interact with people and to be approachable. Winnie was the primary person to raise Sherman Jr. I was not home a lot and she did a great job with him. She loves traveling, in fact, she was my chauffer on long trips and loved to drive. She would drive from Nashville, TN to Las Vegas, Nevada with Sherman Jr. and was very confident about getting on the road and taking off for a particular destination.

Winnie was a good student and Sherman Jr. took after her. She was a celebrity in her hometown, St. Augustine, and loved attending the school reunions there. She was the perfect person for me. She and Sherman Jr. had a life of their own and were not just sitting at home waiting for me. I told her that she should call herself, Winnie Holman Andrus, not Mrs. Sherman Andrus because she was a person in her own right. When I was home, I always attended all of Sherman Jr.'s activities because I wanted to be a part of their lives.

When Sherman came home from Pepperdine, he wanted a new car. He had blown the engine of his 1982 Camaro and they both approached me. Their presentation was quite intimidating, and I was so conflicted that I was stuttering. They began to finish my statements so then Winnie said, "So what you're saying is that this is not the time for a new car?" I said, "Yes!" I left for a concert and when I came home there was a new MazdaMX6 sitting in the driveway. Sherman began to tell me "I promise I'll pay Dad." I knew that I would be paying, and I did. The two of them were in cahoots and had me so bamboozled that I didn't know what to do. They were truly the "Dynamic Duo!"

Winnie was very hospitable. Kids from SNU had free reign at our home. We had people from our hometown come and live with us as they were trying to find jobs at Southwest Airlines. Little V lived with us for a semester as he finished school. We never charged anyone for anything because what was ours was theirs. When I went to California my first job was $49.00 a week and I paid a portion of that to my brother for rent because I was living with him. I loved that our home was always open to others. I think I took on my dad's personality in that respect because he always was giving to others.

We had people from other countries live with us. One man from Brazil and two men from Germany stayed with us for several days and Winnie loved hosting them. I am blessed to have had Winnie in my life for 54 years. She is the most upbeat and happy person I have ever known. I saw that characteristic in her mom, and it drew me to her. I could not have accomplished anything I have done without the complete support of Winnie and Sherman Jr. They were both so self-sufficient that it freed me to minister where the Lord led me.

I haven't been the perfect husband, but Winnie has been the perfect wife. She was always quick to forgive and to understand my shortcomings. If you are interested in finding the right life partner for ministry, you need someone who supports your goals and desires. You must be careful that after you are married, they are not seeking to change you. For example, the guys in The Disciples met their spouses when they were performing on stage. After they were married, the wives complained about their traveling. When I decided to leave Andrae because Sherman Jr. had changed so much in three months, Winnie said, "Don't leave because of what I said or because of Sherman Jr. Stay true to your calling and do what you love." It is the most liberating thing she could have told me! When I decided to go to The Imperials, she did not understand the music or the Southern Gospel scene, but she honored me and left California for Nashville.

It is important that you spend time in prayer as partners in life. We have been married for 54 years and divorce has never been on the table. I don't think I would have made it without her. We had our disagreements just like any couple, but we knew we never were going to live life alone. Even though she is now in a nursing home, I love her more now than on our honeymoon. She needs me now more than ever and I need her more now than ever. We always had fun! Winnie said that she didn't believe she could ever have as much fun as she had with me. If I can make her smile, it makes my day. I am a performer and I performed for her and Sherman Jr. My only regret is that we did not have more children, but God has blessed me with many "adopted sons and daughters" throughout the years.

Where Do Songs Come From?

I began writing songs when I was a young boy. They were not Gospel songs but songs to girls and all that kind of stuff. As I got older, I wanted to write Gospel songs. Andrae encouraged me to write and my first song was *Just Trust In Jesus*. It is amazing where the inspiration for songs comes from. I was watching *The Sound of Music* and the song, *Climb Every Mountain*, just really touched me. From that movie I got the inspiration for *Just Trust Jesus*. It was on our first extended play album when we did Sonata In Soul. It was a testimony that Jesus is in control of our lives. The vocal performance made it special because I sang it with such passion.

I Got Jesus and I'm Satisfied was written when I was in Europe traveling with The Imperials. The song was reggae style, and it was very up-tempo. I was singing the Gospel in a foreign land and it told what I was going through. My songs hit home because they were written about my life at the moment. At that time, the weather was awful, and the song lifted my spirits and it encouraged me.

Here Am I Send Me was written after touring India for several weeks. We stopped in Northern California to do some church concerts and the enemy really had me feeling sorry for myself. Satan said, "Look at you! You've been doing this for over 30 years, and you don't even have the money to go home and see your wife!" I heard another voice ask me, "Why do you do this?" I heard Him say, "Because the fields are white unto harvest." That underscored my commitment to missions and the song flowed.

Caution to The Wind was written just after Andrus, Blackwood, and Company disbanded. The Lord just reminded me that I did not have to be fearful or to be anxious for anything but to seek His will for my life. The song made the statement that I was not afraid, but I was trusting God and throwing *Caution To The Wind*.

Steal Away was inspired by an old Negro Spiritual that talks about going home to heaven. I wanted it to inspire people to steal away to Jesus, knowing that He will keep us until it's time to go home to heaven.

Faithfulness came from a time of personal struggle in my life. I had no place to sing. I had no finances, and I was praying for something to happen. I got a call from Waco, TX and they told me they had a cancellation and wanted me to come and give a concert. They paid all my expenses and as I was landing at the airport the words and the chorus came to my mind and I wrote them down. "Great is Your faithfulness when others soon forget. Your promises are always true, they keep me my whole life through!"

Come Back To Jesus was written for my niece, Diane. She was away from God and I wanted her to know God loved her. "So, you think that no one really cares, when tears fall from your eyes, isn't it time you realized, for those tears the Savior died. And He sees and cares when you are alone and is standing right before you to welcome you back home!"

Everlasting Father was written over several years. I started working on it with ABC, with Karen Voegtlin helping with the chords, and finished it traveling through Alaska when I was moved by the beauty of the passage from Fairbanks to Valdez. Every thirty or forty miles it looked like another part of the world. No way this could come from a "Big Bang!" This had to be created by an *Everlasting Father*! Special thanks to Lonny Bingle for writing the verses!

Witness is on the last album with ABC, *Holiday.* It had a big band and was kind of preachy! I remember that David Baroni, writer of *Soldiers of the Light*, wrote me a letter and told me how much he loved the lyrics. He is a great writer, and I am not in his category, but he was moved by the lyrics. "Don't preach to the rich and forget about the poor!"

Magnify was written because I didn't like the song that ABC used as a first song on the set. Terry said if you don't like it, write something and I did! It had a great instrumental entry that allowed us to come on stage and opens with praise…"We have come to praise the Lord and magnify His Holy Name! We have come to lift our voices and let His praise ring, and if it takes all night long, we're going to praise Him in song."

Think Upon These Things is based on Philippians 4:8KJV. At that time, I tended to think about negative things and hold them in. The Lord convicted me and reminded me of all the great things He hath done and that I needed to think upon things that are good and of good report.

For Such A Time As This is my favorite song and formed in my mind one day as I was working for Integris. I was lost, trying to find the gentleman who needed a ride to the hospital. The lyrics say, "Now's the time to rise up with wings of an eagle. Now's the time to run fast and not faint. I will never leave you nor forsake you. For I am your God, and I am your deliverer. Though men may turn against you I'll be here beside you, for you were born for such a time as this." With all that's going on in the world it reminds me that God is in control.

So, You Want to Be
A Gospel Singer!

You must have the call of God on your life because Gospel music is a difficult field. It is more than making a living, it is about serving others. Lately there have been artists in Gospel music who have made a lot of money. That was not the case when I started. There is nothing wrong in making a good living through whatever vocation or avocation that you choose. However, ministry in Gospel music is about giving more than receiving. I have been sustained over the years because God has used me to touch lives. It has not been a great deal of financial remuneration. Invariably I receive messages, texts, phone calls or letters from people who let me know that my songs and ministry have made a profound difference in their lives, even years ago.

The first step in being a Gospel singer is to commit your life to Christ. That means following His leadership and allowing Him to guide your path. You need to have a personal life of prayer and surround yourself with Godly people who will pray for you and help hold you accountable. You need others who will join you in praying for God's will and direction in your life. It is better to have the counsel of Godly people than to have a manager or a booking agent who may or may not have a personal relationship with Christ. Scripture says, "Seek first the Kingdom of God, and His righteousness and all of these things shall be added unto you." (Matthew 6:33KJV)

In a practical sense, you should always read your contract. That may seem funny, but just because a company produces Christian recordings, it does not make them a Christian company. When we had contract negotiations with recording companies, they always brought legal representation with them. We had none. When we finally brought one in with us, they said, "You guys don't trust us?" The onus was always on us. If we brought representation with us, it meant that we were not solid Christians according to them. One time in negotiations I brought a tape recorder and put it in the middle of the table. They didn't like that too much. They made lots of verbal promises, but they didn't come through with what they promised. Do not sign away your power of attorney! Keep all rights to your music and lyrics!

Throughout my career I have always been willing to sing wherever God opened doors. I know things have changed a lot since then, but I still believe that is a good practice. Many times, pastors or members of large congregations have seen me in smaller venues and have subsequently invited me to their church because my performance was not based on the size of the audience. I give 110% every time regardless of the number of people listening. My motto is simple: "Love God! Love His People!"

Find a ministry that you believe in and support it. I started ministering through Teen Challenge. From there I did prison ministries on my own. Don't let everything be about being paid for everything you do. I still do things for my community. Every year in Bethany, OK there is a Bethany Freedom Festival. I participate every year and enjoy reconnecting with people I have known over the years. I believe it generates good will for me within the community and beyond.

Generally, artists or groups want to create a nonprofit ministry. I am neither for nor against it. I did not do that because I wasn't truly "nonprofit." I paid my taxes and I paid into Social Security and that is probably the best thing I ever did. I get a very substantial Social Security check every month and am most grateful. Many ministers and ministries opt out of Social Security, but it has been a blessing for me and Winnie.

Finally, live what you sing about! No one is perfect but bad news travels much faster than good news. Try to be above reproach. I have had many rumors started about me, most of it has been generated out of thin air. When I first started, people imagined stuff and shared it with others. I would hear about it down the road. It is like people look for things to disagree upon. I don't agree with a lot of preachers; it is not so much as what they say, but all about how they live their lives. Why do you need a $10 million dollar home? You should be known more for your philanthropy, than how big your house is. There is nothing wrong with making a good living, but we must be better than the world. You might call me a "Pollyanna", but I believe if we really supported the poor and did not preach so much division, we wouldn't need a welfare system. We should be looking for places where we agree, not disagree, and focus on what God want us to do and who He want us to be. Sometimes I feel like we hate the sinner more than we hate the sin. That is completely wrong. The way to reach the lost is to love them to Christ. Love God! Love People!

Final Reflections

At the time of this writing, we have over 500,000 deaths due to the COVID-19 outbreak. Our country is more divided than it has ever been in my lifetime. I believe that as the Body of Christ we have lost a great opportunity to reach the masses. We have allowed Black Lives Matter to define the times pertaining to racism. I thought that after all these years the church might redeem herself from her shameful past regarding racial injustice. From my perspective, it seems that too few Christians have been in the forefront in the fight for racial equality and justice. If the church were true to the Word of God, there would be no need for BLM. In Luke 4:18 it says "The Spirit of the Lord is upon me because He has anointed me to preach the Gospel to the poor. He hath sent me to heal the brokenhearted, to proclaim deliverance to the captive, and recovery of sight to the blind, to set at liberty those who are oppressed."

As a young Christian I often prayed and hoped that someone would come to our defense. No one did. All of these great men of God who now share in every election "10 Reasons to Vote For ….a Mormon….or a corrupt businessman….have been silent. In 2012 Franklin Graham stated emphatically that he could vote for a Mormon (Mitt Romney) but not a Muslim (Barack Obama). Conservative radio host, Joe Walsh, also called President Obama a Muslim. He has since apologized but not Franklin Graham. Because of his declaration I lost a lot of "friends." I asked them how they could extrapolate from any of President Obama's actions that he was a Muslim. He did all the other things that the presidents did before him. After President Obama was elected for a second term, another friend posted on Facebook; "Get ready for the Judgement!" In other words, we finally made God angry by electing a black man as president! We drove the Native Americans off their land; we owned slaves; we had Japanese in internment camps; however, the tipping point to incur the wrath of God was electing a black president twice. Really????

I recently had an acquaintance email me and ask me how I felt about Black Lives Matter and why was it necessary to use the term, "African American." I took my time to respond to him because I was angry, hurt, and insulted at his inquiry. I shared with him that if the Church of Jesus Christ had been all it should be there would be no need for "Black Lives Matter" because in essence, to God, all lives matter. I also shared with him that we chose to use the term African American because it was much better than the other names, we had been called which were very demeaning and denigrating. African American is a term that depicts pride in race and country. He must be unaware that we also use the terms; Native American, Hispanic, Mexican American, Latino American, or German American when we wish to express pride in both who we are and where we live. It is this type of thinking that saddens me because of the ignorance or simply the refusal of other people to see beyond themselves. I don't believe he meant to be insulting, but he was.

I genuinely believe the church has lost its moral compass. It seems to me that we are losing young people under the age of forty. They see our hypocrisy! The marches, not only in the United States, but all over the world, demonstrating against the savage killing of George Floyd, have been attended by more whites than blacks.

My co-author and friend, Peggy, recently challenged me to really explain what systemic racism was in my world and thinking. So, I did my research so I could adequately give a good definition of systemic racism, also known as institutional racism. Systemic racism is a form of racism that is imbedded as a normal practice in a society or organization. It can lead to such issues as discrimination in criminal justice, employment, housing, health care, political power, and education. Harvard professor, Harvey Mansfield, writes in the Wall Street Journal that the phrase incoherently describes the society that is so little racist that no one can respectably advocate racism. Yet so much racist that every part of it is soaked with racism. We live with a paradox of a racist society without racists. I shared with her that throughout my whole life I always felt like I had to be better than my white counterparts, work harder, perform better, like I was always trying to prove myself. I was paid less because I was black (by white Christians no less), and at times I was not permitted to use the same entry as The Imperials until staff was informed, "Yes, he is with us...let him in." I even had a white pastor tell me recently that when his congregation found out I was black, he either had to cancel the concert or find a new church. Today? You ask...still today? Yes, still today. I also want to share that most of my career has been spent ministering to predominately white congregations with wonderful people who have loved me and my family and supported us with prayer and with finances. I am not saying that all white evangelicals are racists I don't believe that they are! I just want you to know my heart and realize that from my standpoint the church of Jesus Christ has failed to fulfill His commandments with all people and that racism is still alive and well. It may look different; a little more sophisticated...a little less direct...but it still exists, and it is breaking our country apart. I also want to acknowledge that racism exists on both sides. I realize that there are people of other races who are very antagonistic towards white people and paint all of them with the same brush. I do not want to do that. I think the black church has historically been on the forefront of fighting racial injustice however there are areas of prejudice in the black community against white people that need to be acknowledged and addressed. Everyone needs to be working together to bring us together as a nation of one people, regardless of race, creed, or color. For instance, Whitney Houston was booed at a Stellar Awards event even though she was the most successful artist of that year. The black audience booed her because they said she was "too white." For many years black artists' music was considered to be "race" music and was not played on non-black radio stations. There were many complaints about that. Whitney broke through that barrier and she was ostracized for selling lots of music to her white listening audience. I just think that racism is ignorant, and we need to work together to eradicate it. I am thankful for all the people God has brought into my life regardless of their color. He has used a variety of people to help me become the man of God that I am today All of us need each other and it makes a difference when they are God's blessings in your life.

As for me, and my house, we will serve the Lord and continue to make a difference for Him wherever he opens doors! My prayer and hope remain that somehow, some way, His church will take up the battle for injustice and equality for all people and be on the forefront for fulfilling the mission of Christ that I shared from Luke. I am committed to that and I pray you are too.

I want to extend a heartfelt thanks to the following individuals who have made such a difference in my life with their prayers, finances, and friendship. God has blessed me with you, and I am eternally grateful!

Jim Andrus, and Barry, Quinn, Bryan, Nicole, Robin, and Courtney Andrus
Miles Andrus
Lynn Andrus
Jaxon Andrus
Jim and Norma Ashmore
Connie Berlin
Larry & Linda Bishop
Denisha Blackmon
Lisa Byers
Jason & Celeste Chavarria
Bruce Christian and Mike Shelton of Woodland Hills Baptist Church
Elmer & Lucille Dade (with special thanks to Lucille for helping me get started on writing my book)
Dan & Sylvia Dillard
Dove Ministries
Lloyd & Jill Duplechan (My nephew and wife and my number one fan and ardent supporter)

Margaret Leopold Marge Duplechan (My sister) for all her support through the years

Dr. Lester Duplechan, and wife, Dr. Hermelia Sweatt Duplechan

Lauren Freeman

Allen and Tena Gibbs

Midia Rivera & Sergio Gonzalez

Pastors Alan and Miriam Humphries

Kellie Larson

Willie Leopold Jr. and Cookie

Sam and Naomi Lopez

Gerald Leopold, World Class Guitarist

Roland & Carol Majeau

Jason Leopold, World Class Bassist

Mitch & Diane Mason

Ed McConnell

Anna McIntosh

Steve & Kay Mock

Kenny Mock

Betty Neale

Eric Obubusa & family

Mark & Lauren Pickens

Shirley & April Porter (My sister-in-law and niece)

Paula Rae Hayes Sparks

Aaron & Diana Stanfill (My best friend and wife)

Linda Van Horne

Johnny & Donna Stevens

Rex & Karen Voegtlin

Rev. John Walker

Donnie Williamson & the Williamsons

All the pastors who have allowed me to minister to your congregations over the years.

Special thanks to Cathlyn Acker and Marilyn M. Stark for their editing skills

I'm sure I have missed some names but those listed above must buy ten books and if I missed your name, you are in luck!

Sherman Andrus Sr.

Albums and Videos

It's Gonna' Rain	Andrae Crouch and Sherman Andrus	1965
He Took My Sins Away	Andrae Crouch and Sherman Andrus	1965
Come and Go with Me	Andrae Crouch and Sherman Andrus	1965
Prayer Is the Key to Heaven	Andrae Crouch and Sherman Andrus	1965
EP 45		1968
Take The Message Everywhere	Andrae Crouch and The Disciples	1967
I've Got Confidence	Sherman Andrus	1968
The Imperials	The Imperials	1972
The Imperials Live	The Imperials	1973
Follow The Man With The Music	The Imperials	1974
No Shortage (Grammy and Dove Awards Winner)	The Imperials	1975
Just Because	The Imperials	1976
The Very Best of The Imperials	The Imperials Compilation	1974
The Imperials Featuring Sherman Andrus and Terry Blackwood		1979
Soldiers of the Light	Andrus, Blackwood, and Co.	1980
Following You	Andrus, Blackwood, and Co.	1972
Soon Coming	Sherman Andrus	1976
Grand Opening	Andrus, Blackwood, and Co.	1977
How The Years Pass By	Sherman Andrus	1978
ABC Live	Andrus, Blackwood, and Co.	1979

Step Out of the Night	Andrus, Blackwood, and Co.	1982
Holiday	Andrus, Blackwood, and Co.	1984
Caution To The Wind	Sherman Andrus	1987
Seize The Moment	Sherman Andrus	1988
Sherman Andrus Live, Hit Me Band	Sherman Andrus	1994
Ode To Hawaii	Sherman Andrus Compilation	2004
Merry Christmas	Sherman Andrus	2006
A Servant's Heart	Andrus and Bingle	2013
Think Upon These Things	Andrus and Bingle	2003
For Such A Time As This	Andrus and Bingle Live	2018
The Best of Andrus, Blackwood, and Co.		1983
Show Me	Musical by Jimmy and Carol Owens	1971
Come Together	Musical by Jimmy and Carol Owens	1973

Produced:

Sounds of Christmas	Peggy Stark-Wilson	1989
Trust His Heart	Peggy Stark-Wilson	2002
Love Explosion	Karen Voegltin	1981
He's My Leader	Karen Voegltin	1983
Misty Morning	Karen Voegltin	1979
On The Road to Soldatna	Miriam Humphries	1990
Raindrops	Miriam Humphries	1995
Rest In Me	Miriam Humphries	2005

Co-Author:
Dr. Peggy L. Stark-Wilson

Dr. Peggy L. Stark-Wilson

"I have had the privilege of knowing and loving Sherman and Winnie Andrus for nearly fifty years. God wonderfully allowed our lives to intersect when I first began teaching at Boynton, OK and continued when I moved to San Antonio, TX. During the past year Sherman and I have worked on constructing his life story while laughing, reminiscing, and marveling at how God has miraculously moved in his life over the years. It has been an extraordinary privilege for me to be a part of such a historic and inspirational project. I thank God that He has enabled us to construct this amazing story into a warm, inviting, thought provoking book for others to enjoy."

Dr. Peggy L. Stark-Wilson attended Olivet Nazarene University, Trinity University, and Texas A & M University. She served as a teacher, principal, and district school administrator in

San Antonio, TX for 35 years. Peggy has been active in leadership in the Church of the Nazarene and served on the Board of Trustees for Southern Nazarene University for more than 30 years and on the Board of Trustees for Nazarene Bible College for 20 years. She has authored one other book that was self-published, *Eighty + Ways To Say, "Thank You", Expressing Appreciation In The Workplace! We Are Better Together!* Peggy resides in the Texas Hill Country with her husband, Rev. Roger L. Wilson.

Endorsement:
Sandi Patty, Grammy and
Dove Award Winner, Gospel Artist

When you are a young artist in the 1980's you remember those more seasoned artists who have gone before you and who have been kind to you as you begin what God has for you to do. I will always be grateful and thankful that Sherman Andrus has been one of those guiding lights along my path. You are going to love his story…his honesty and the authenticity from which he has been able to sing the story of God's faithfulness!

And on a serious note…thank you Sherman for being so kind to a new young artist. You'll never know what your encouragement through the years has meant to me. Sandi

Endorsement: Jon F. Stemkoski, Founder and President of Celebrant Singers

Sherman Andrus is one of the finest men I know, and one of my longest and dearest friends. And wow, can the man sing! Nobody can question that. He's got very few peers in that department.

But that's only the tip of the iceberg of who Sherman really is, as this long-awaited book will reveal. I think the best and most accurate thing that can be said about Sherman is that he's the real deal. He's one of the most solid, honest, sincere, and thoroughly pure-hearted Christians I've ever met. There's no guile in his heart. His only desire in the 50 years I've known him, has been to honor and glorify Jesus through his life and his music.

This book takes us through his childhood in rural Louisiana, the many experiences God used to shape him, his love story with his wife, Winnie, the heart-wrenching pain of losing their only child to cancer, and his iconic journey of music and ministry as a soloist and with some of the top Christian musicians of this generation. It's a veritable banqueting table of miracles, an eye-opener to a large slice of contemporary Christian music history, and most importantly a vibrant testimony to God's faithfulness throughout the mountains and valleys of his incredibly fruitful life. Sherman's seen it all, and through this amazing must-read book, we are privileged as readers to share his journey with him.

Endorsement: Lonny Bingle, Gospel Artist, Song Writer, and CEO, Lonny Bingle Ministries

Proverbs 18:24 "A man of many companions may come to ruin, but there is a friend who sticks closer than a brother (ESV)." Proverbs 18:24 "Friends can destroy one another, but a loving friend can stick closer than family (GW)." This verse reflects Sherman and me in my mind. Sherman and I first met at an Andrus, Blackwood and Company concert when I was in the Navy in 1977. It was one of their first concerts as ABC and Sherman was very gracious after the concert in speaking with me. I knew that one day I wanted to do what he was doing. After my discharge in from the Navy in 1981, I became a Pastor and started full-time ministry. Sherman and I had stayed in touch and then in 1982 I began promoting concerts. I would have ABC in as a part of those concerts. We briefly lost touch at the end of the eighties, but in 1996, Cindy Korcnek, from Vashon Island, got us in touch with each other again. I immediately invited Sherman to come and minister at my church in Spokane. When Sherman was inducted into the Gospel Music Hall of Fame in 1998 for both Andrae Crouch and The Disciples and The Imperials, I had him come to the church. We surprised him with a nice hotel, limousine service to the church concert and a red carpet to welcome him to the church. Over the next several years our relationship continued to grow and then in 2001, I invited Sherman to go on a mission trip with us to India the following year. He graciously accepted and went with our mission team. On the way over I proposed that we start a new singing group. I could tell he was completely underwhelmed, but I was persistent. We ended up writing several songs on that trip and Sherman introduced the group the Monday after we returned on TBN. We finished our first recording in 2002 at my brother Karl's studio (Mission Control Records). After that we began our first tour in Alaska with Pastor Gary Morton at Anchorage 1st Assembly of God. Since 2002 we have developed a close friendship and have experienced the ups and downs of ministry together. Sherman has been a great confidant, mentor, and friend. We have had a blessed time together since 2002 and are not finished yet. Together we have recorded three albums with "A Servant's Heart" garnering the attention of the Grammy committee. Our new "LIVE" Blu-ray will be coming out shortly after this book and we are looking forward to God's continued blessings as we do our best to love Him, each other, and those to whom we minister. There are so many things that could be shared, but suffice it to say, I love Sherman's steadfast love of the Lord, his creativity, and insights. I have witnessed him as he has ministered both through song and as a teacher encouraging those around him to be strong in the Lord and the power of His might (Ephesians 6:10). We have traveled the world together and ministered in several nations in Europe, Africa, Asia, and North America. Sherman is one of my closest friends and has embraced my wife Kim and all my children and their families as well. It is my sincere pleasure to add my endorsement recognizing Sherman's decades of service to our Lord and Savior Jesus Christ.

Endorsement:
Dr. Kevin McAfee, Hollywood Film Maker

Sherman Andrus has lived a life others can only dream about. As one of the most talented musicians and vocalists his early career skyrocketed in all areas of commercial music and Christian contemporary music. However, landing a background vocalist for Elvis: The Concert the greatest entertainer in American music singing with The Imperials propelled his career into the highest level. Not only did Sherman break all barriers as an African American singer in an all-white group, but he also became a heralded talent in all of Gospel Music. While winning numerous music awards, singing for State Governors, and performing the National Anthem at National Championship Basketball games, Sherman has left an indelible impression on all who have contacted his life. What is most impressive about Sherman, has been the love he always has exemplified for family, the integrity his life and his undeniable character. He is a man of missions, a man with a powerful message of hope and he is beloved to every audience he has been asked to serve. Sherman is not only an amazing artist, but he is also one of the Godliest men I have ever known. I feel honored and blessed to endorse this exciting book and will be recommending his book to everyone in the film industry where I have served since my young adulthood. Since our team has been making motion pictures, we have been impressed with Sherman's unique voice and his ability to be a powerful communicator for his faith

Endorsement: Todd Thurman Director of Athletics Metropolitan State University of Denver

I've known Sherman Andrus since 1987. This was the year that I started my coaching career at Southern Nazarene University and where Sherman was the men's basketball team's chaplain. We became close friends quickly, which lead to Sherman singing at my wife and I's wedding. His performance was one of the highlights of our special event.

As the years went by, Sherman was always a great mentor and friend to the team, my family and for me personally. After 31 years of an amazing marriage, my wife Lynne passed away from Ovarian Cancer. For her funeral, my family and I couldn't imagine not having Sherman there to sing for her. When we called him, he didn't hesitate for one second and agreed to be there. In Sherman's way, he was able to take a very devastating moment and make it into a celebration of life. I always say that Sherman was there to lead us at the beginning of our journey and was there when it was time for my wife to go her heavenly reward.

Sherman is a great man that I and my family will always appreciate, love, and admire. Thank you, Sherman, for all you mean to me, my family and everyone that you have touched.

Endorsement: Bob Hoffman
Head Men's Basketball Coach
Central University of Oklahoma

I am proud and honored to endorse an autobiography written by Sherman Andrus. Known as an acclaimed vocal artist, few may know of the behind-the-scenes ministry of this incredible man. As a college coach, Sherman spent years pouring into the lives of my college athletes, helping shape who they are today. He went on road trips, as well as overseas mission trips with us. I consider him a great friend to this day, and I highly recommend the reading of his new book.

Printed in the United States
by Baker & Taylor Publisher Services